EXPERIMENTAL ECO→DESIGN

ARCHITECTURE / FASHION / PRODUCT

A ROTOVISION BOOK

Published and distributed by RotoVision SA
Route Suisse 9
CH-1295 Mies
Switzerland

RotoVision SA
Sales and Editorial Office
Sheridan House, 114 Western Road
Hove BN3 1DD, UK

Tel: +44 (0)1273 72 72 68
Fax: +44 (0)1273 72 72 69
www.rotovision.com

10 9 8 7 6 5 4 3 2 1

ISBN: 2-88046-817-5

ART DIRECTOR Luke Herriott

DESICN Cara Brower (New York, New York)
and Zachary Ohlman (Kentucky / Paris)

PAPER STOCK This book is printed on Stora Enso
matte art. This paper is produced from logs
derived from well-managed forests and / or
plantations, as endorsed by the Forest
Stewardship Council.

Printed in Singapore by Star Standard
Industries (Pte) Ltd

EXPERIMENTAL
ECO→DESIGN

ARCHITECTURE / FASHION / PRODUCT

CARA BROWER
RACHEL MALLORY
ZACHARY OHLMAN

RotoVision

CONTENTS →

00—
INTRODUCTION
Where We Begin

We all know that our environment's resources are limited and that our world's natural balance has become disrupted. Toxins and byproducts from manufacturing not only harm our environment, but also our health. We are a consumer-based culture with a desire for the next best thing. This desire for new products isn't going to change—it is built into our modern way of life. The key to a sustainable future lies in finding a way to satisfy our current society's lifestyle in a more constructive manner. **Experimental Eco-Design** considers economic, environmental, and social values in production, life cycle, and choice of materials.

How can design make a difference? Design is an eternally evolving and changing force. There are endless developments in materials, techniques, and processes, not to mention new design trends and styles. The notion of integrating ecological awareness into design practices is becoming more of a concern and a necessity. Designers play a key role in the advancement of these practices because they are responsible for making the vital material and production decisions for consumer products. Designers are not only stylistic innovators, but also problem solvers. Whether you call it sustainable, environmental, green, or eco-friendly, this forward-thinking frame is beauty with brains. **Experimental Eco-Design** considers how design will impact on the world in which we live.

It takes an informed designer to implement change, and one with the enthusiasm to break boundaries and forge new directions. This book aspires to be an exciting and accessible resource that brings together a global range of environmentally and socially responsible writers, thinkers, designers, and companies. They illustrate how we can create solutions that live with the world, not just in it. These designers use the refuse of yesterday to create a stylish product for today, considering its lifespan and degradability to protect the environment tomorrow.

Thinking with an eco-design frame of mind shouldn't involve an entirely new way of designing, but it does require new ways of thinking about design. The works collected here are as diverse as the designers who've created them. The idea that unites them is their consideration for eco-friendly methods along with visionary style. They are all experimenting, pushing in new directions, and reinventing old ideas. They are all at the forefront of a positive design movement.

LOOKS GOOD, FEELS GOOD, IS GOOD?
EDWIN DATSCHEFSKI

You've just designed a new product or completed a new project. The client's happy, it all looks shiny and new, and you're feeling pretty pleased with yourself. But stop and think for a moment. Is there more to it below the surface? Recently, while working on a project, we started to trace the wood. We discovered that it had been illegally logged in Cambodia by a rogue army faction that rounded up villagers and forced them to work on the felling and log extraction. The wood was then sent over the border illegally to Vietnam, where child laborers were used to process the pieces. The final product then appeared on sale in a well-known retail store, at a bargain price.

There's also a problem with end-of-life design. All products are destined to wear out, break, or become unfashionable. What's going to happen then? Have you designed the product to be repaired or disassembled, with all plastic parts correctly labeled for recycling?

Every material and component, from wood and steel through to aluminum and carbon fiber, has an environmental story behind it. Usually it is a tale of effluent, pollution, and scarred landscapes, of poisoned water and health hazards for workers. I call all this the "hidden ugliness" behind an otherwise beautiful-looking product. Yet no one is drawing your attention to these things.

It's really down to designers to make a change. Your clients expect you to have worked out all the safety, ergonomics, and quality issues, and they should be able to rely on you to chase up environmental matters as well.

Is your work destroying ancient landscapes and paying for some corrupt general's new limo? Or is it made of wood from a highly biodiverse natural forest, handcarved by Finnish monks, and lovingly varnished with organic linseed oil? Could you tell the difference? It takes a bit of thought and research. It requires you to care about the provenance of the materials and components you specify.

Both designers and consumers are starting to think beyond the way products look and perform and to consider what goes on when products are made and what happens when they are eventually disposed of. They recognize that while an award-winning chair may look beautiful, it cannot represent the pinnacle of mankind's genius if it is made using polluting methods or by exploiting workers. Even the Scandinavian-style minimalist interiors that seem so pure and clean have this hidden ugliness—formaldehyde in the plywood and mdf, hexavalent chromium pollution from tanning leather, and damage to communities and the landscape from mining the pigments used in white paint.

There is an urgent need to make all industrial products and processes sustainable—beneficial for people, profits, and the planet. The good news is that there are hundreds of interesting and innovative new products—plastics made from cornstarch, totally nontoxic upholstery fabric, ultra-low energy lighting, recycled computers, and solar offices—and information for designers on sustainable choices is starting to become available.

NATURAL LAWS

If we learn from nature and change the quality of the energy and materials we use, then we can move closer to being fully sustainable. For example, if we use solar energy, there may be no environmental impact at all, so we could use as much as we like or could afford. Another important idea is that the flows of materials in nature tend to be cyclic, so you can never run out of resources. By recycling more minerals we can mimic nature. And obviously, using materials that have been grown is also a good thing—there are now some very high-tech and high-performance plastics made from corn as well as wood and soya biocomposites to choose from.

It is very achievable to undertake design for mass production that follows the basic protocols followed by natural systems. The five design requirements of sustainable products are that they be: cyclic, solar, safe, efficient, and socially responsible. The first three mimic the protocols followed by plant and animal ecosystems.

CYCLIC

The product is made from compostible organic materials or from minerals that are continuously recycled in a closed loop. This can be achieved by making use of recycled metal, glass, and plastic, and by creating products that are more recyclable. For example, the company Milliken Carpets takes back used carpet tiles and then cleans and repatterns them to give the tiles a new lease of life. Emeco makes incredibly durable chairs from aluminum that has an 85-percent recycled content. These chairs are also completely recyclable as they are simply left matte or polished. Cyclic products can also make use of grown materials such as wood, leather, wool, or one of the new bioplastic materials made from corn and potato starch.

SOLAR

The product, in manufacture and use, consumes only renewable energy that is cyclic and safe. This includes wind, small-scale hydro and solar energy—there has been a boom in solar panel manufacturing recently. Some factories are run using these various forms of renewable energy. In many cases, the bulk of energy used during a product's lifetime is expended during its manufacture.

SAFE

All releases to air, water, and land provide food for other systems. Every manufacturing process is considered and its negative impacts reduced or avoided entirely. For example, Foxfibre is a naturally colored cotton that grows in rust, green, or red and so needs no dyes.

EFFICIENT

This requirement is based on the need to maximize the utility of resources in a finite world. The product in manufacture and use requires 90-percent fewer materials and 90-percent less energy and water than products providing equivalent utility did in 1990. Using less is always a good idea. One clever example is the SoftAir Inflatable Chair, which uses 85-percent less material than a conventional chair.

SOCIALLY RESPONSIBLE
All companies have an impact on the people who work for them and the communities within which they operate. Without stringent checks, you may find that your product or some of its components and raw materials are being made with child labor or even forced labor, or that employees are forbidden to participate in trade union activities. The manufacture and use of sustainable products should support basic human rights and natural justice. This means ensuring decent working conditions and fair pay, ideally with a social "premium" to be used by the producers to improve their living and working conditions. Nonfood examples of good social sourcing include Deep E Co footwear, which has a direct partnership with rubber tappers in Brazil.

WHAT NEXT?
The goal of sustainable design is to make all products 100-percent cyclic, solar, and safe. Designers must look to a future in which everything is completely compatible with nature. The question should always be "Is this designchoice moving us in the right direction?"

Edwin Datschefski helps people figure out how to make their products sustainable.
He has developed a set of free, Web-based educational resources, which people in 36
countries are using to learn about sustainable design. Go to http://www.biothinking.com

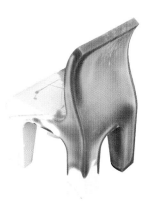
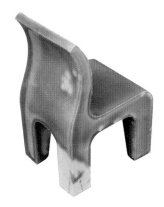
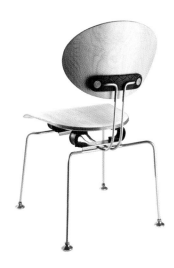

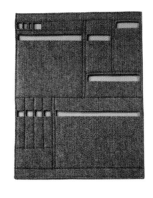

01-
TRANSFORMING MATERIALS

Shigeru Ban Architects / Kazutoshi Amano and Shinichi Sasaki / Anne Bannick and Lene Vad Jensen / Alyce Santoro / Tom Dixon / Mio / Bart Bettencourt / Emiliano Godoy / Remarkable / Bless / MetaMorf / Ukao / Annemette Beck

Inevitably, all design has a limited lifespan, whether it becomes redundant, breaks, or simply becomes outdated. As much as we'd like to put these items out of mind once they're discarded, their mass must reside somewhere. Considering low-impact materials is vital. Renewable materials (those that return to the earth as easily as they are harvested), nontoxic materials (those that have replaced chemicals in their manufacturing process with safer, natural ingredients), and easily recyclable materials (those that do not contain mixed compounds) are all intelligent options. The goods in this section have all been enhanced through sound and informed selection of materials.

A NEW FRAME OF MIND
PETER DANKO

A NEW DESIGN STYLE
You are about to witness a quantum leap in design and the decorative arts of a magnitude not seen since the advent of the Bauhaus movement in the 1920s. The event is the birth of a design style embracing the marriage of sustainability with industrial production. I call this style Eco-Modernism.

The Bauhaus movement articulated a unified design esthetic, a comprehensive mental model to embrace the ethos of the industrial revolution. This evolved from a multitude of disparate design philosophies that emerged as reactions to the industrial revolution during the previous century.

Today, even the most conservative person recognizes that our resources are finite and that careful consideration must be given to the processing of our waste. So how do we alter the mental model of our culture to build a sustainable world society? The foundation has already been laid by the US Green Building Council and the LEEDS sustainability criteria (created by the US Green Building Council). The more challenging and exciting answer to this question comes with the esthetic realization of these principles in industrial design and the decorative arts.

CHANGING VALUES
The furnishings we choose reflect who we are—our values, our heritage, and where we fit in the social hierarchy. The issue of sustainability has recently become a consideration when we choose products. Sustainability, however, will never be the sole key to the success of a product. As always this will be its design and how it reflects our values. So, in order to become a sustainable society, our values need to evolve so that we perceive products from a different frame of reference.

The Chesca chair can be used to illustrate how our furnishings changed in the past as a result of an evolution of values to a different frame of reference. This famous tubular steel chair was designed by Marcel Breuer in the early 1920s, during the time of the Bauhaus movement. Steel chairs were being made before, but the designs and structures of chairs prior to the emergence of the Chesca chair reflected the natural world: a branch of a tree, for example. Breuer's chair not only reflected the industrial process that produced the chair, it also honestly reflected the unique properties of the material itself by using a cantilever to illustrate steel's unique structural ability.

THE DESIGNER'S ROLE
As a designer of sustainable furniture, it's my job to create compelling designs in the hope they will inspire people to choose sustainable design over safer, more traditional designs. In the late 1970s I began making ply-bent and molded plywood furniture. One of the attractions that prompted me to build my first bending machine to experiment with ply-bending wood was the medium's ultra-efficient use of resources. Crafting furniture from layers of hardwood veneer yields 9-10 times more usable wood from a log than making furniture from hardwood lumber.

To produce many ply-bent chair designs, only 15 percent of the wood from a log is lost to waste. When using solid hardwood, on the other hand, as much material is lost to waste as is required to make the lumber alone. The average waste it takes to make a finished solid hardwood chair is 150-200 percent more wood than is used in the chair itself!

Other aspects of my attraction to ply-bending were my sense of the medium's ability to make wonderful free-flowing shapes, its fascinating structural properties, and its warmth as a natural material. Further, the creative potential of this material is still largely unexplored, having been plumbed by a mere handful of designers, most notably Alvar Aalto and Charles and Ray Eames.

THE NEED FOR RECOGNITION

The craft of working solid wood has been around since Neolithic times. Over millennia, craftsmen from many cultures have developed techniques to form rich traditions and many styles of furniture. The skill of working wood in this conventional manner is rooted in human culture; our concept of conventionally made wood furnishings is an integral part of our heritage and is highly valued.

By contrast, the technology to economically craft veneer into solid shapes has been with us a little more than 100 years, and furniture crafted with these techniques is not much more than 70 years old. This medium is so new that some collectors would not even consider such works to qualify as antiques. Furthermore, I do not know anyone in academia who has focused their attention on the development of ply-bending as a technology and marked the progress of its evolution into styles, and its status as an art and a craft.

My goal is to elevate the perception of ply-bending and its capacity to create a look and a style that is both compelling and exclusive. I want to erase the popular misconception that plywood is largely a utilitarian medium, to help people to see ply-bending as an integral part of our culture and heritage, and to raise its status in our society.

Many designers and artisans today are applying their talents toward producing Eco-Modernist designs. Like the art and craft of ply-bending, their designs ask us to shift our perception of beauty to a different frame of reference. When these Eco-Modernist designs receive the combined and sustained recognition of educators, museum curators, entrepreneurs, and ultimately the popular media, then Eco-Modernism will become a sustained and an integral part of our culture.

PAPER ARCHITECTURE →

WHAT: Japan Pavilion
WHO: Shigeru Ban,
Nobutaka Hiraga, Shigeru
Hiraki, Jun Yashiki
WHERE: Japan
MATERIALS: Paper tubing
and timber
QUALITIES: Low-impact
deconstruction, easily
recycled

Japanese architect Shigeru Ban has literally built a body of work founded on an inventive use of overlooked materials, creating objects and structures and solving problems with surprisingly untraditional materials—paper, cardboard, and bamboo.

When commissioned to design the Japan Pavilion for the 2000 Hannover Expo, Ban and team were given the task of reflecting on the theme of environmentally related problems with an environmentally conscious solution. The solution was to design a 'paper pavilion,' a structure formed solely from the surprising strength of recycled paper tubes. Acknowledging the environmental impact and lifespan of the materials, Ban and team created an architectural story of construction, demolition, and recycling for this temporary structure.

The completion of a building is usually thought to be the end of the project, but the Paper Pavilion completes its story after demolition: its materials are chosen for their low-impact and ease of recyclability.

<u>WHAT: Paper House</u>
<u>WHO: Shigeru Ban</u>
<u>Architects</u>
<u>WHERE: Japan</u>
<u>MATERIALS: Paper tubing</u>
<u>QUALITIES: Low-impact</u>
<u>deconstruction, easily</u>
<u>recycled</u>

Ban's Paper House is another example
of his architectural fascination with
paper tubing. In this the traditional
Japanese house is recreated through
the simple beauty of a traditional
material used in an untraditional way.

01 Japan Pavilion
02 Paper House
03 Paper House detail

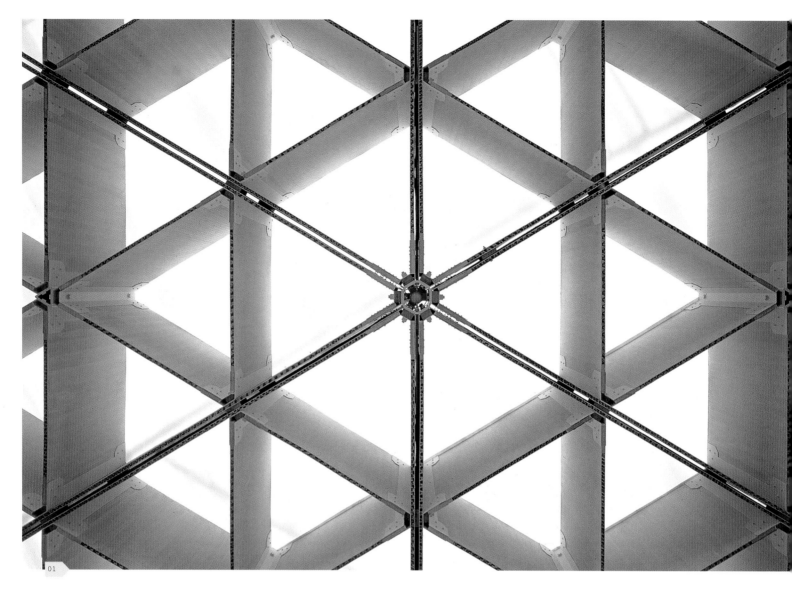

01

WHAT: Nemunoki Museum
WHO: Shigeru Ban
Architects
WHERE: Japan
MATERIALS: Paper
honeycomb lattice frame
and steel column
QUALITIES: Low-impact
deconstruction, easily
recycled

Nemunoki Gakuen is located in a valley in Kakegawa City at a site deep in the mountains between a tea field and a flower garden. In this valley, where streets are forgotten behind the luscious green of nature, there was an attractive triangular site. The Nemunoki Museum was created as a meeting ground where children could exhibit their paper art works. What better material to use for such a

facility than paper itself? Lightweight and collapsible for ease of transportation to the site, with surprisingly strong structural properties, Ban's choice of material provided the perfect fit. Honeycomb-shaped boards with a surface membrane glued to the rib structure worked effectively as a durable and inviting structure, with diffuse light created by the structural design.

01 Nemunoki Museum detail
02 Nemunoki Museum interior

CARDBOARD SEATING →

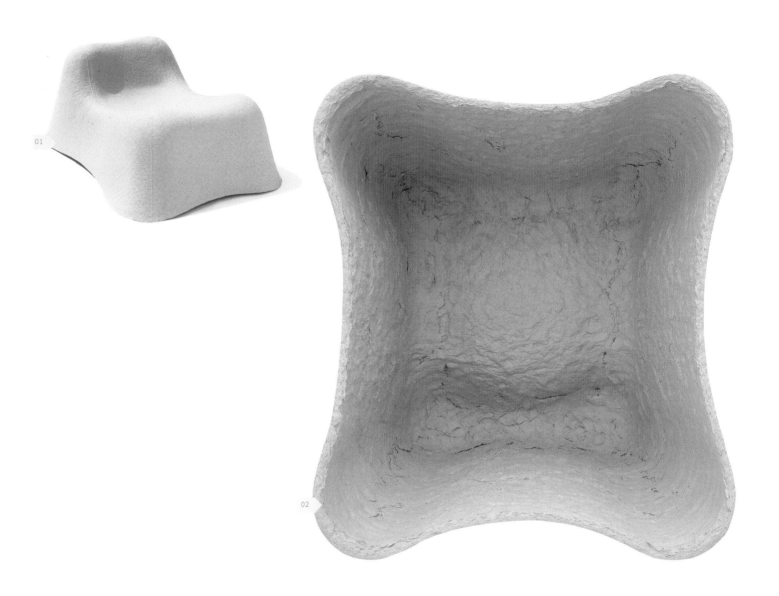

01

02

WHAT: Mould Chair
WHO: Kazutoshi Amano and
Shinichi Sasaki
WHERE: Japan
MATERIALS: Cardboard pulp
QUALITIES: Low-impact,
lightweight, easily
recycled

The Mould chair was formed by
Kazutoshi Amano and Shinichi Sasaki,
who collaborated to create a line of
products made from 100-percent
recycled cardboard pulp. The Mould
project seeks to enhance this
material's unique character while
remaining true to the concept of
biodegradation; when no longer
required, this chair can simply
return to the soil.

Mould's material comes from 100-
percent recycled cardboard boxes,
using the same production process as
that used for standard egg cartons.
In the case of egg cartons, the pulp
solution is formed and hardened using
specific molds, but Mould products are
currently created by hand.

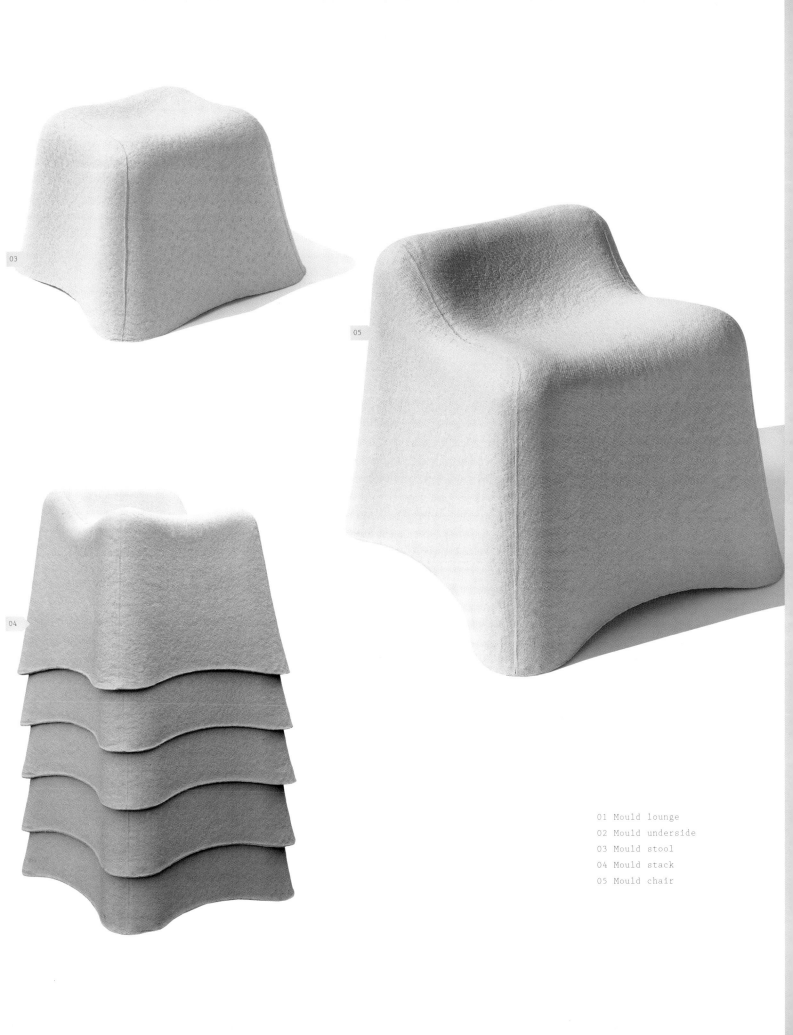

03

05

04

01 Mould lounge
02 Mould underside
03 Mould stool
04 Mould stack
05 Mould chair

DISPOSABLE TABLEWARE →

01

24/25

WHAT: Papcorn
WHO: Anne Bannick and
Lene Vad Jensen
WHERE: Denmark
MATERIALS: Wheat, corn,
and lactic acid
QUALITIES: Renewable
resources, biodegradable

Created by Anne Bannick and Lene Vad Jensen, this ultra-hip everyday dinner set is compostible, formed with renewable materials such as wheat, corn, and lactic acid. These material components are not only readily available, but as they are naturally derived they are virtually harmless at the end of their life cycle. With disposability in mind, all of the Papcorn products have a limited environmental impact from beginning to end—they follow part of nature's own cycle.

02

03

01 Sushi set

02 Papcorn is light, flexible,
   and compact

03 Dinner set complete
   with spork

RECYCLED FABRIC →

01

02

WHAT: Sonic Fabric
WHO: Alyce Santoro
WHERE: United States
MATERIALS: Woven audiotape
QUALITIES: Recycled materials

Sonic Fabric is an imaginative concept that came to life through the weaving together of actual audiotape with polyester thread. Inspired by Tibetan Buddhist prayer flags—by which printed mantras are released to the world and carried by the wind—Alyce Santoro's creations are made from found ambient and spoken-word recordings woven on a traditional loom. The added bonus, discovered after the fabric's creation, is that this material can be heard; by running a tape head over the fabric you can create audible sounds.

For its stage debut, Sonic Fabric was worn by Jon Fishman, a friend of Santoro's, and drummer for the rock band Phish. Fishman's garment was created from his collection of over 250 cassette tapes and woven into a garment reminiscent of his trademark orange, donut shape-patterned garbs. The creation was worn onstage and 'played' by Fishman with custom tape-head gloves, to create DJ-like scratching rhythms.

03

04

01 Fish dress
02-03 Sonic dress
04 Sonic fabric detail

RECYCLABLE PLASTICS →

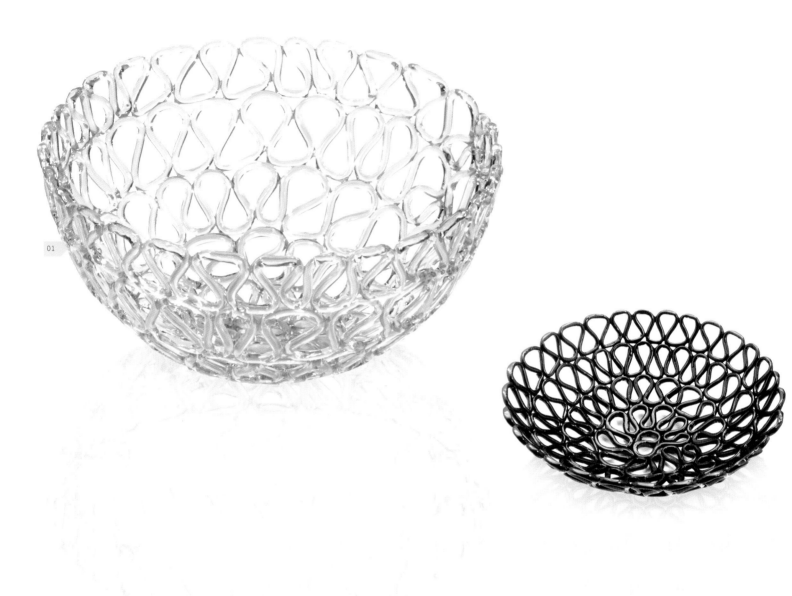

01

WHAT: Fresh Fat series
WHO: Tom Dixon
WHERE: United Kingdom
MATERIALS: Eastman Provista
QUALITIES: Recyclable, nontoxic

Tom Dixon began his fascination with design exploring the decorative and structural potential of recycled materials and industrial scrap. Dixon's design has always involved a hands-on approach, with each piece evolving as a built form, requiring no need for design sketches. The Fresh Fat series in no exception. With this he has created imaginative, extraordinary handmade objects from Eastman Chemical Company's Provista,

a material chosen for its rugged yet delicate look and environmental consciousness; it is nontoxic and can easily be recycled. Each glistening product is created from warm, spaghetti-like extrusions of plastic that are woven, twisted, and molded to create exquisite handmade bowls, light shades, and one-off furniture pieces which have the added benefit of an engaging manufacturing process—customer interaction.

'Fresh Fat Plastic started as an
experiment in future retailing.
If out-of-town shopping, where the
consumer goes direct to the warehouse,
is the present state of shopping, then
surely the next step would be to have
the customer go straight to the
factory. The customer is then involved
in making their own product.'

01 Fresh Fat bowls
02 Fresh Fat chair
03 Fresh Fat table

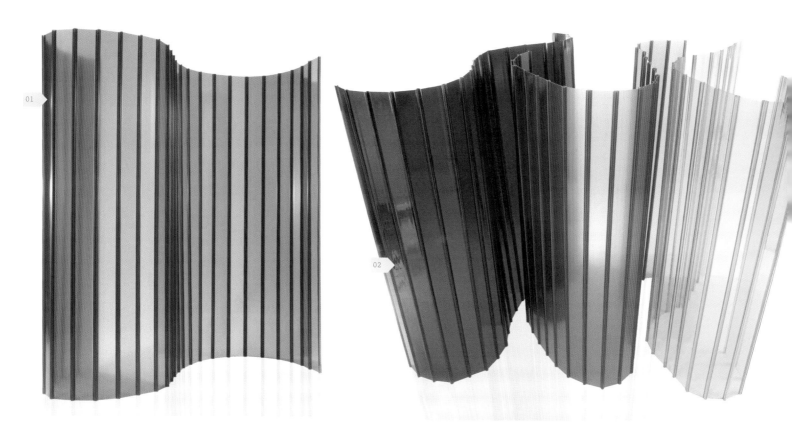

"Materials—we want to know everything about them.
Where they come from, how you work with them, how
far you can push them, what else you can make from
them. And we like them thicker, more generous, and
simpler than most."

WHAT: Extendable Screen
WHO: Tom Dixon
WHERE: United Kingdom
MATERIALS: Eastman Provista
QUALITIES: Recyclable, nontoxic

A spin-off from the Fresh Fat
experiment is the architectural
room divider, also made from Provista.
It uses the knowledge Dixon gleaned
from the extrusion process to make
a unique and extendable piece of
mobile architecture.

01-03 Room divider

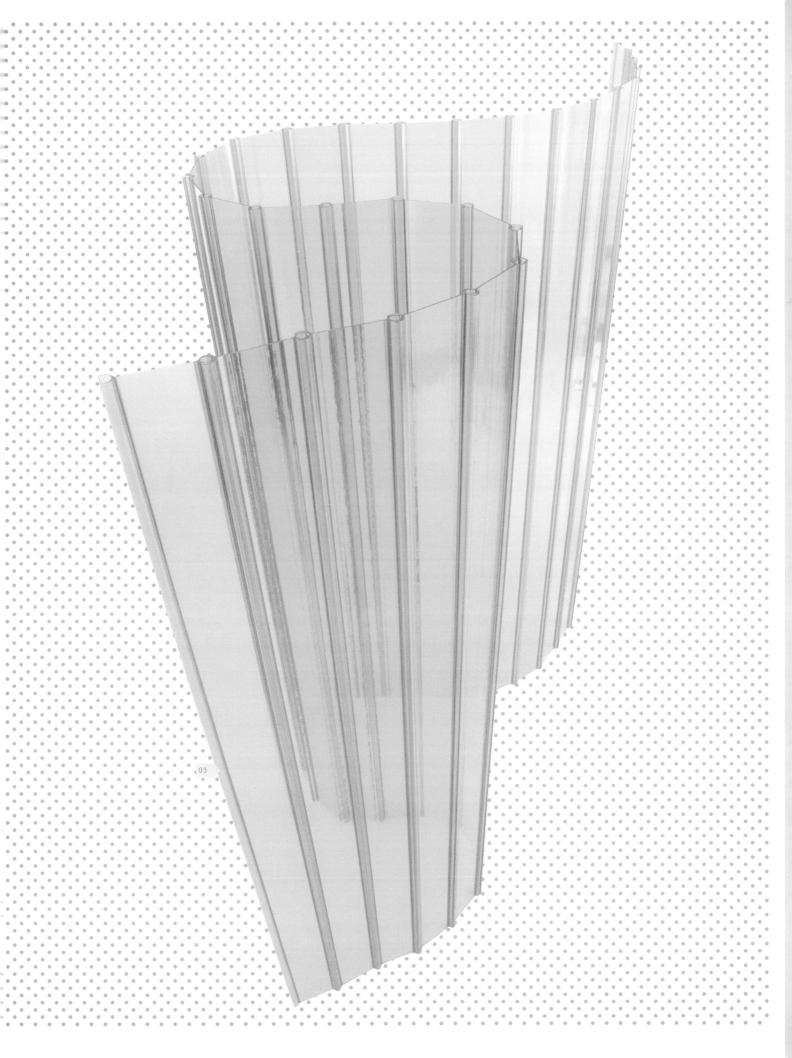

03

CAFE TABLES AND TABLEWARE →

01

02

WHAT: Cafe stone series
WHO: Tom Dixon
WHERE: United Kingdom
MATERIALS: Red Jaipur
sandstone, green marble
QUALITIES: Recyclable,
nontoxic

The Cafe stone series is an original example of Dixon's fascination with raw materials. All the objects were formed from the earthy beauty of red Jaipur sandstone or green marble.

01 Cafe stone table,
   green marble
02 Cafe stone table, red
   Jaipur sandstone

"The products represent the desire to strip away any superfluity to reveal the underlying characteristics of the production process, exposing the intrinsic nature of each object."

WHAT: Ecoware
WHO: Tom Dixon
WHERE: United Kingdom
MATERIALS: Bamboo-fiber plastic
QUALITIES: Biodegradable

Ecoware was created from plastic reinforced with bamboo fiber. Naturally formed materials return back to the environment at the end of their life cycle, which makes them an ideal choice for the series.

01 Eco cup stack
02 Eco cup

LIFESTYLE PRODUCTS →

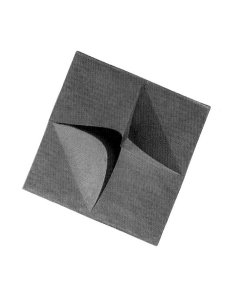

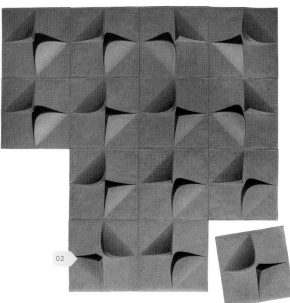

WHAT: V2 Wallpaper Tiles
WHO: Mio
WHERE: United States
MATERIALS: Recycled post- and pre-
consumer waste (PVC)
QUALITIES: Recyclable

WHAT: Capsule Light
WHO: Mio
WHERE: United States
MATERIALS: Wool, steel wire, energy-
efficient and compact electrical
components
QUALITIES: Recyclable, energy efficient

Mio is a design studio that set out to create "eco-intelligent" interactions, products, services, environments, and culture. Tagged the MioCultureLab, the studio has a diverse mix of creative individuals who share the desire to create beautiful and eco-friendly products for everyday use.

V2 is a reconfigurable, 3-D wallpaper tile that provides more than just a creative visual solution for plain and boring white walls. Referred to as adaptive architecture, V2's versatile patterns are easy to install and adapt for almost any wall or ceiling. Made from 100-percent post- and preconsumer waste paper (PVC), V2 allows you to customize the look, feel, and acoustic properties of your walls. The concept lies in finding new meaning and appreciation for urban waste by redefining it as part of your personal environment.

The Capsule Light explores wool's natural beauty and ability to diffuse light, and can be used to create many effects. Composed of molded wool, steel wire, and electrical components

03

04

WHAT: Grid wall pockets
WHO: Mio
WHERE: United States
MATERIALS: Recycled felt
QUALITIES: Recycled materials,
natural materials

(an efficient compact fluorescent
light), the Capsule Light is designed
for ease of disassembly and recycling.

Aiding in the use of vertical space, the
grid wall pockets are ideal for storing
magazines and books as well as small
items such as pens and other supplies.
Fabricated from die-cut and stitched
recycled felt, these poster-size pockets
add personality and function to the
walls. The beauty of this product is
that it transforms recycled materials
into a storage unit for useful items
that often appear as clutter on a desk.

01 Capsule Light
02 V2 Wallpaper tiles
03-04 Grid wall pockets

BAMBOO FURNITURE →

01

02

36/37

WHAT: Bamboo furniture
WHO: Bart Bettencourt
WHERE: United States
MATERIALS: Plyboo
QUALITIES: Renewable resources,
biodegradable

Bart Bettencourt likes to experiment with a diverse range of materials when designing and crafting his range of contemporary furniture. Designed with minimal geometric lines and forms, he has experimented with such ecologically friendly materials as Environ, Dakota Burl, and BIOFIBER wheat composite. Environ uses soy-based resin to bond agricultural waste and recycled paper products into solid and composite sheets. Dakota Burl uses waste sunflower seed husks to form a unique product that resembles authentic burled wood. BIOFIBER wheat uses the same

technology with wheat stems as the main ingredient. Plyboo, a Bettencourt favorite, is a plywood made from 100-percent bamboo. A registered material of the Smith & Fong Company in San Francisco, California, all the woods used are harvested by hand from managed forest lands, which minimizes environmental impact. The adhesives used in the laminating process emit no detectable toxins.

Since bamboo is a grass and not a tree, it can be cut off near the ground and will regrow from the same roots.

03

04

05

06

It does not require replanting and the living root systems shore up soil and prevent the destructive effects of erosion caused by traditional lumbering. All Bettencourt products are handcrafted in his Brooklyn studio.

01-02 Bamboo dresser
03-04 Bamboo and stainless
     steel chair
05 Bamboo chair
06 Bamboo dresser

MOLDED SUGAR →

01

02

03

WHAT: Sweet Disposible
WHO: Emiliano Godoy
WHERE: United States
MATERIALS: Sugar
QUALITIES: Renewable
resources, biodegradable

Disposability is sweet for Emiliano Godoy, whose Sweet Disposible products experiment with matching object lifespan and material longevity. Sugar is crafted to form short-term, environmentally friendly materials for various objects such as coat hangers and golf tees. By using both durable and nondurable products with a 100-percent biodegradable material, the disposal of the product is taken into the realm of design: every product will eventually be discarded so why not consider the end result as the prominent design focus?

The materials used include sugar, cream of tartar, water, and food coloring where color is required—all completely biodegradable and natural. After molding, the pieces are left to dry. No extra energy is used for this; they are simply stored in a dry place for a few hours.

The sugar's crystalline structure gives it surprising strength. Crystals of different sizes are arranged in such a way—small nestling between medium nestling between big—that minimal air is left between them.

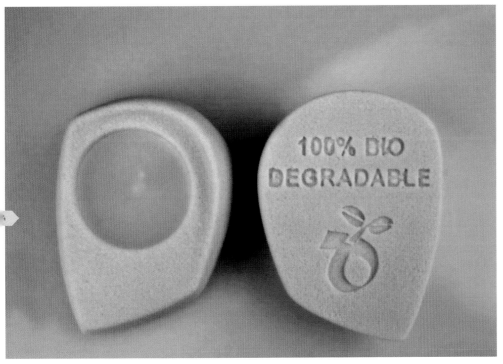

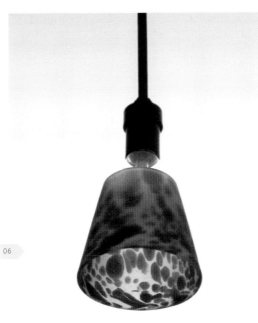

Water is used as the binder for molding and when this evaporates, the mix tends to shrink, which creates an extremely solid piece.

Surprisingly, the sugar material created doesn't melt. It only dissolves in water, which is what makes it truly disposable. Pieces can last for years. Their surface doesn't get sticky with time nor does it attract insects.

01 Coat hook
02 Golf tee
03 Candle
04 Candle top and base
05 Lamp
06 Hip lamp

<u>RECYCLED</u> <u>STATIONERY</u> →

"If people can see recycling happen in an innovative, creative way, they are much more likely to recycle in their everyday lives."

THIS PENCIL IS MADE FROM ONE RECYCLED VENDING CUP

01

<u>WHAT</u>: Remarkable pencil
<u>WHO</u>: Remarkable
<u>WHERE</u>: United Kingdom
<u>MATERIALS</u>: Recycled
<u>vending cups, computer</u>
<u>printers, tires</u>
<u>QUALITIES</u>: Recycled
<u>materials</u>

Remarkable is the British brainchild of Edward Douglas Miller, an environmentalist and former manager of a plastics factory. His remarkable creation is a pencil made out of a recycled plastic vending cup. In its London factory, Remarkable is now producing over 20,000 pencils per day. This means that 20,000 plastic cups are being saved from landfills every day.

Branching out beyond pencils, Miller has expanded the Remarkable range to include a number of other stationery items, including mouse pads, notebooks, and, most recently, pens made from recycled milk cartons. All these products are made using only waste and environmentally friendly materials. They are true to their tagline, "Turning junk into something Remarkable."

01 Colored pencils
02 Punk Metal series
03 Lava Sky computer pens
04 Lava Sky series

REAPPROPRIATED CLOTHING AND FURNITURE →

01

02

WHAT: Clothing and
furniture
WHO: Bless
WHERE: France, Germany
MATERIALS: Found objects,
wool, leather
QUALITIES: Recycles and
reappropriates materials
and found objects

Bless, German duo Desirée Heiss and
Ines Kaag, create clothes, furniture,
and clothes for furniture (not
furniture covers, but genuine
chairwear). The designs range from the
basic to the sophisticated, but all
have a relaxed look. The Bless
collections are eco-friendly; the duo
often use recycled fabrics or reuse
objects to make new ones. N°19:
Uncool, the key piece of this
collection, utilizes a special

knitting process. Using yarn made
of different threads mixed together,
Bless created a "growing" effect,
with the knitting getting bigger and
bigger from sleeve to collar for
a sweater, for instance, or from
fingertips to elbow for a pair of
gloves. Their Found Object Project
(umbrella and leather socks) presents
an alternative to designing; it alters
found objects to adapt them for use
as clothes and accessories.

01-02 No.19: Uncool

03 No.8: Found Object Project,
   leather socks

04 No.22: Turban

05 No.2: Disposable T-shirts

06 No.20: File chair

07 No.8: Dripless umbrella

PLASTIC OUTDOOR FURNITURE →

01

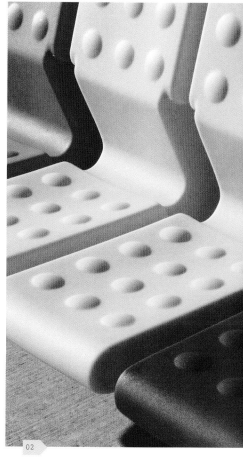

02

WHAT: Tempo outdoor
furniture
WHO: MetaMorf
WHERE: United States
MATERIALS: Recycled
plastic
QUALITIES: Recycling
discarded materials

During the late 1990s and early 2000s, Colin Reedy, of MetaMorf, has been transforming the soda bottles, yogurt cups, and plastic grocery bags you threw out last week into playful and engaging plastic furniture. Combined with a colorful vision reminiscent of a child's toyland, Reedy's work finds the ground where the natural and artificial can come together through materials—design.

Experimenting with design processes and manufacturing, Reedy's focus has been new solutions for recycled plastic—often an overlooked and underrated material. "By now, most people have been exposed to recycled plastic in some shade of brown and fabricated as picnic tables, bus or park benches, fences, or maybe a parking bumper … but it can be beautiful. Plastic bends, plastic can be colorful. Please use its qualities!"

03

04

His Tempo line of outdoor furniture solves two social issues—plastic waste and public seating—with one colorful design solution. Tempo benches not only add style to the urban landscape, they are also modular, cost effective, and even graffiti resistant. Reedy doesn't scimp on efficient materials either—Tempo benches use 100-percent plastic waste from consumer and industrial sources, which is something that makes Reedy proud. "All over the world, people and governments are looking for solutions to plastic waste. I'm putting together a package that offers the direct use of plastic waste in a community by turning it into local street furniture. I'm excited about this effort because I feel plastic waste is a public problem and transforming it into street furniture offers a very public solution. And no, they won't be available in brown!"

01-03 Tempo outdoor
      furniture series
04 Recycled plastic pieces
   at Reedy's workshop

BAMBOO FURNITURE →

01

02

WHAT: Dreyfus and Yolanda
series
WHO: Ukao
WHERE: United States
MATERIALS: Bamboo
QUALITIES: Renewable
resources, biodegradable

Ukao is the creation of Gerard
Minakawa, a designer with a passion
for surfing and bamboo furniture.
The word Ukao (pronounced yoo-kay-oh)
means "way of life" in Swahili, and
represents Gerard's drive to find
creative solutions that can live in
harmony with the world in which we
live. Ukao actively pursues its vision
of blending contemporary style with
traditional, ethnic materials,
particularly bamboo.

In Asian-Pacific cultures, bamboo has
been regarded as a multifunctional
material, to create structures,
furniture, clothing, and even food.
Unlike traditional hardwoods, bamboo
grows at a rapid rate and can be
harvested for decades from the same
roots. As a natural material, it has
low-environmental impact at the end
of its life cycle.

01, 02, 05 Yolanda side chair
03 Dreyfus end table
04 Yolanda side chair detail

TACTILE TEXTILES →

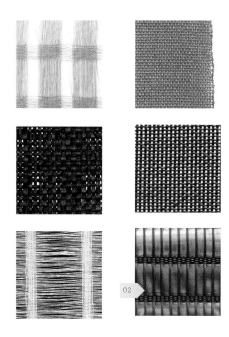

"The philosophy behind my design is to simplify the design as much as possible, to remove what is unnecessary so that only what is essential remains. To make a clean, clear, and sharp design by way of carefully controlled fantasy."

48/49

WHAT: Textile Design
WHO: Annemette Beck
WHERE: Denmark
MATERIALS: Paper, yarn, wool, felted wool, silk, felt, cotton, copper, plant fibers, rubber, bicycle tubes
QUALITIES: Natural materials, recycled materials

Annemette Beck creates beauty with the unexpected. Her Danish studio produces unusual and one-of-a-kind upholstery fabrics, rugs, curtains, blankets, and room dividers. What makes her textiles extraordinary is the combination of natural materials such as paper, yarn, wool, felted wool, silk, cotton, and copper, with peculiar materials such as plant fibers, rubber, and bicycle tubes. Rugs are made with knotted wool, hand-tufted wool, rya techniques, papertwine both flat and double weave, with the reverse image on the other side. Last but not least, she produces rugs from bicycle tubes. For wall hangings, she uses delicate, natural materials such as metallic thread, Arenga fiber, and horsehair with sticks and twigs for dividers. Beck's textiles transform any room, giving a decorative and textural atmosphere through a very natural and sophisticated approach to design.

04

01 "Silver" room dividers,
   woven in silver threads and
   light wire
02 Fabric details in paper,
   yarn, wool, felted wool,
   silk, cotton, copper,
   plant fibers, rubber, and
   bicycle tubes
03 Double weaving in wool at
   the Danish Embassy in
   Beijing
04 Prism room dividers
   in paper yarn

EFFICIENCY BY DESIGN

easyGroup / LOT-EK / Richard Hutten / Pepper-mint / Ben Wilson / Peter Hancheck / Dave Kuene / Superhappybunny / Erik Newman / Whirlpool / Sean Godsell Architects / Designframe / Luceplan / Truck / Artcoustic / Bless / Bart Bettencourt / Emiliano Godoy / Michael Jantzen / Kisho Kurokawa Architect & Associates

Efficiency is an eco-friendly quality that cuts down on energy used whether in production, transportation, or use. For manufacturing, efficiency means using less materials and labor to produce the object itself. In form, efficient design uses simpler elements, which creates less labor during the manufacturing process. Lightweight objects that can be disassembled and packed flat create ease of transportation, and allow more pieces to be shipped at one time. Modular components rely on constructing objects from a single form. Individual modular pieces can be used in multiple formats, with the ability to interlock and create a diverse range of formations. Objects can also be designed to save energy by harnessing it from renewable sources (such as the sun), or by conserving the amount of energy used.

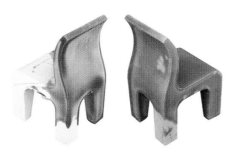

CREATIVE COMMUNITIES
EZIO MANZINI

SUSTAINABILITY AS DISCONTINUITY

We all have to learn to consume fewer environmental resources. We need to create new forms of community, from the local to the planetary level. In this way we will be able to make the transition toward sustainability.

The idea that we can live well by consuming fewer resources and generating a sense of community is completely opposite to the model that industrial society has so far generated. On a global level, comfort and well-being are generally linked to increased consumption. This means that it is not possible to take significant steps toward sustainability using existing ideas and methods.

Great systemic changes—macro-transformations—are generated by micro-transformations, that is, from the radical innovation of local systems. The observation of these micro-transformations can help us to envisage some of the aspects of the new system that will emerge in the future.

This article focuses on some significant micro-transformations oriented toward sustainability that are taking place in contemporary society. It points to some of their characteristics and discusses what designers can do to take on an active role in their development and diffusion.

AN UNSUSTAINABLE PROSPERITY

The consumer lifestyle that industrial society has developed as a general model is in crisis: the planet is not big enough to sustain a world of 6 billion people at today's levels of consumption. Today, 20 percent of the world population consume 80 percent of the resources of the planet, while 80 percent of the world population consume only 20 percent of the resources. If the 80 percent want to adopt the models of consumption so widely and powerfully promoted by contemporary industrial society, they will not find the resources to do so. There is insufficient air, water, energy, and territory for 6 billion people to consume on the model of the richer countries. This environmental pressure also creates political tensions. The dual ratios 80/20 and 20/80 express, in an unequivocal form, the desperate need for alternative lifestyles and proposals for how to live on this planet.

A BLOCKED SYSTEM

In face of the mounting evidence of problems created by our ways of life and production today, contemporary society appears to be a blocked system; companies and politicians say they cannot do anything because "the people" do not want to change. In turn, individuals and communities, even if they express the will to change, say they cannot do anything because "companies" and "politicians" do not offer any alternatives. Designers also find themselves in this paralyzing game, blocked inside a dynamic that does not permit them to imagine anything but new and useless gadgets or, at best, incremental improvements in a system that is intrinsically unsustainable.

To unblock the system, we first need to adopt a different representation of reality. Instead of considering the people, the companies, and the politicians as entities, we should see them as what they are: groups of individuals with different positions, which are often contradictory. If we adopt this new representation of reality, the profile of the world appears much more varied and dynamic and less intransigent. With this shift in perception, we observe that although there are worrying phenomena, there are also more positive signs, which point to the possibilities of other ways of being and doing. These unconventional ways could be the seeds from which new ideas for lifestyles, production, and economies can grow.

CREATIVE COMMUNITIES

For example, we can see ways of living, such as community housing, in which space and services are shared in order to improve quality of life. There is the development of products that utilize local resources and capabilities but that are connected to wider global networks. A variety of local initiatives to promote healthy and natural nutrition exist, from the international movement "Slow Food" to the diffusion in many cities of a new generation of farmers' markets. There are cooperative services for the care of children, for instance, "micro-nests" (small crèches promoted and managed by the parents themselves), and care for the elderly, such as the "living together" initiative, which integrates old and young people in the same space. We see new forms of socialization and the exchange of favors, including Lets—the Local Exchange Trading Systems—and the Time Banks. Alternatives to the monoculture of the individual car have developed, from car sharing and car pooling to the rediscovery of the potential of the bicycle. Networks of direct connection and fair trade between producers and consumers, such as fair trade initiatives, are diffusing on a global scale.

These varied cases of social innovation have fundamental traits in common: they are all radical innovations by local systems. They contradict acquired ways of doing and introduce different and intrinsically more sustainable ways. For example, advanced systems of sharing spaces and equipment where individual use of space normally dominates are being organized. The quality of healthy and organic foods is being rediscovered in contrast to the norm of consuming mass-produced foods. Inclusive systems of service have been developed, as opposed to the normal way of supplying these kinds of services, which anticipates the total passivity of the users.

There are other common features. All of these promising cases are the result of the initiative of people with a talent for particular design capabilities who have focused on particular objectives and found appropriate tools to achieve them. These inventive and entrepreneurial people did not wait for an overall change in the system (the economy, institutions, or large infrastructures). They have used what is already there to produce something new. If we accept the statement by the French mathematician Henri Poincaré that "creativity is uniting the preexistent elements in new useful combinations," these active minorities can be defined as creative communities.

These creative communities are all profoundly rooted in one place; they base themselves on local resources and, directly or indirectly, promote new forms of socialization. At the same time, they are connected to networks of similar initiatives on an international scale, so they can compare their experiences and share the problems. The communities are therefore local entities but also cosmopolitan. What is of interest is that they propose solutions that combine the interest of the individual with social and environmental interests, and therefore have the potential to be genuine sustainable solutions.

These creative communities show us that it is already possible to take steps toward sustainability. Also, by providing concrete examples of what could be "normal" in a sustainable society, they nurture social discussion and the generation of shared visions on this theme. At the same time, they point to new market possibilities in the development of sustainable solutions.

It is interesting to note that the cases and communities described can be found in all the areas that can be defined as urban in the historic cities, in the emerging cities, in the large urbanizations and also, even though with some different characteristics, in the favelas and bidonvilles, and in all the human conglomerates without name that make up the new planetary metropolis.

Certainly, creative communities are still the initiatives of a minority, but these minority initiatives are spreading and are assuming the profile of a vast cosmopolitan building site: a dynamic and varied ensemble of individuals and communities with the intention to build concrete hypotheses of possible futures.

PROMISING CASES AND NEW QUESTIONS
Let's look at pragmatic aspects of these projects and to what extent the promising cases of social innovation, and the creative communities that generate them, can be the stimulus for the systemic innovations and the laboratory for the development of a new generation of products and services.

For example, can the experiences of sharing residential services (cohousing) be the starting point for a new generation of equipment for domestic and residential functions? The service infrastructure for a residential and productive polycentric system includes the distribution of power grids, yet in order to manage the infrastructure, systems for the generation and management of complex partnerships are also required, as well as a support system for evolved forms of participative democracy. Solutions that enable healthier, more natural nutrition and a direct relationship with the producers can give a new direction to the entire food industry. Localized products and self-production may involve productive processes that are specifically conceived and can be adopted in other areas of the food industry.

These cases of social innovation not only satisfy immediate demands for products and services, they also ask a profound question about a possible redirection of the system of production and consumption. In fact, the organizational models, and in some cases at least, the business models that the creative communities propose, can point to lines of research and development for new, appropriate organizational and technological platforms. Design, which is a practical activity but is also part of culture and research, can make a huge contribution not only to the design of products and services that the creative communities require, but also to the development of more general transformations in industry.

MODULAR HOTEL →

01

02

WHAT: easyHotel
WHO: easyGroup
WHERE: United Kingdom
MATERIALS: Fiberglass
QUALITIES: Modular design
allows high quality with
low cost

easyHotel makes finding an affordable
and comfortable room for the night,
well, easy. Part of easyGroup, a
British venture including rental cars,
cinemas, and an airline, the core
concept is to create a modular hotel
design that is also low-cost,
innovative, and fun.

The design includes interior elements
that are consistent in quality and
recognizable to their guests.
Durability, as well as esthetics,

have been paid great attention in
order for the rooms to have a longer
life span. The modular design format
allows for easyHotel rooms to have the
flexibility to exist in a variety
of shapes and sizes in any location.
Each private room contains a shower
unit, lavatory, and at least one
double bed. Due to this modular
construction, the easyHotel creates a
comfortable (and affordable) temporary
living arrangement that is easy to
construct, manufacture and maintain.

01 easyHotel, entrance
02-04 easyHotel, private room

MOBILE ARCHITECTURE →

01

01 American Diner exterior
02 03 American Diner interior

58/59

WHAT: American Diner
WHO: LOT-EK
WHERE: United States
MATERIALS: Shipping containers
QUALITIES: Transportable, modular
design, multiple functions

LOT-EK is a design studio that blurs the boundaries between architecture, art, entertainment, and information through the manipulation of by-products used in our industrial/technological culture. LOT-EK uses prefabricated objects, systems, and technologies as raw materials to create unexpected spatial and functional solutions. For today's increasingly transient culture and lifestyle, LOT-EK has created contemporary dwelling solutions that

are efficient in design and use of materials, and easy to transport (by any means) due to their expandable and modular components. LOT-EK's interpretation of the classic American Diner is conceived by simply coupling to sea containers, leaving a gap in between for a row of stools. Designed to be fully converted and furnished in the US, then shipped to Japan, the American Diner brings a cultural icon to other shores in efficient and low-maintenance fashion.

WHAT: Mobile Dwelling Unit
WHO: LOT-EK
WHERE: United States
MATERIALS: Shipping Containers
QUALITIES: Transportable, modular design, multiple functions

With the Mobile Dwelling Unit (MDU) project, LOT-EK proves that the possibilities of modular transformation are endless. A Mobile Dwelling Unit is created from a singular shipping container. Cuts in the metal container walls create easily expandable subunits, each encapsulating one living, working, or storage function.

The MDU also takes standardized worldwide shipping into consideration, as each subunit can be packed into another, much like a Russian nesting doll. This transportable, modular, low-maintenance unit is perfect for an urban lifestyle with continuously changing needs.

01, 03-04 MDU interior
02 MDU exterior

CONCEPTUAL FURNITURE →

01

WHAT: Zzzidt-objects
WHO: Richard Hutten
WHERE: The Netherlands
MATERIALS: Polyethylene
QUALITIES: Multi-functional, minimalist design

02

Creating conceptual and functional furniture, product, interior, and exhibition design out of his Eindhoven design studio, Richard Hutten has been a key component of the experimental design collective Droog since its inception in 1993. Hutten's creations rely on the philosophy of not giving set solutions to his design audience, but possibilities. People can use his objects in the way that they want to.

Zzzidt-objects are a prime example of
this philosophy at work. Originally
designed for the Centraal Museum in
Utrecht, the Zzzidt objects are
furnishings meant to be placed
throughout the garden for visitors who
desire to sit outside. Inspired by his
son's seated bouncing ball, the idea
for a lightweight, multifunctional,
mobile piece of furniture was created.
Zzzidt can be used as a stool or
table. The handle makes it easy to
carry, and also doubles as an ideal
place for your drink.

01 Zzzidt-objects
02 Zzzidt doubles as a
   playful object
03 Zzzidt handle/cup holder

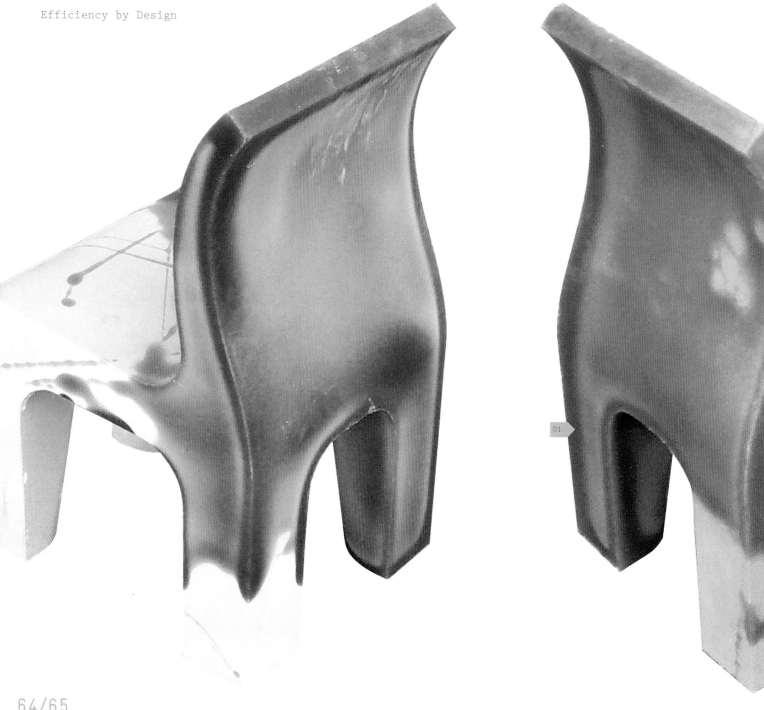

64/65

WHAT: Bronto children's
chair
WHO: Richard Hutten
WHERE: The Netherlands
MATERIALS: Two-component
plastic
QUALITIES: Long life span

The idea behind the Bronto children's
chair was to form a chair in one
piece, with a soft exterior (so
children wouldn't hurt themselves), but
that was also strong and long-lasting.
A custom molding machine was developed
to form the Bronto chair, for which
two-component plastic, rather than
industrial thermoplastics, was used.
Every chair's form is unique, with its
own irregularities. This automatically
makes Bronto a very personal and
sustainable object—one worth keeping
and passing down through generations.

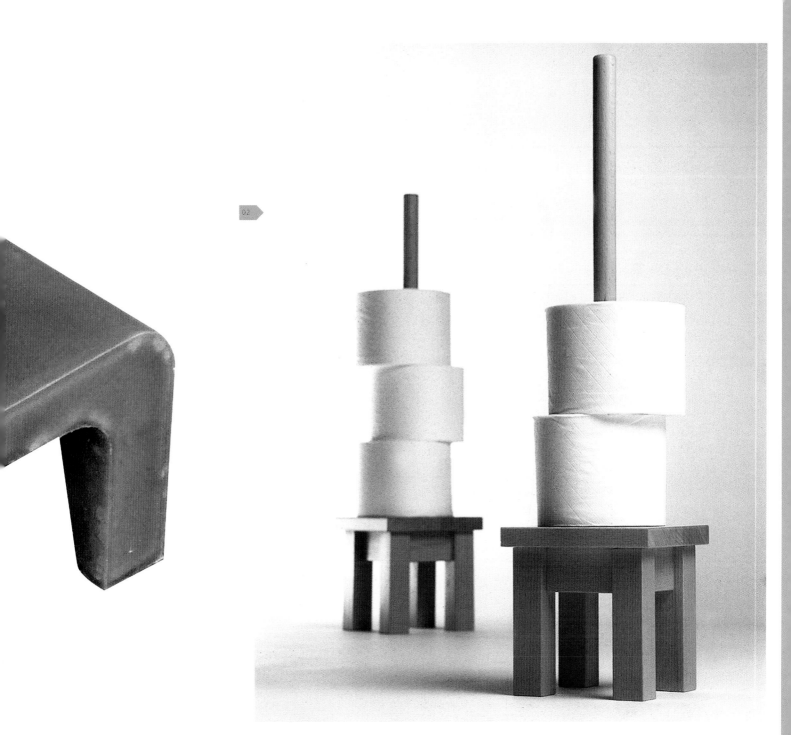

02

WHAT: Lootable
WHO: Richard Hutten
WHERE: The Netherlands
MATERIALS: Maple or beech
QUALITIES: Minimal use of
materials

Hutten's Lootable is a powerful example of functional and minimalist design at its best, complete with conceptual twists. Made from maple or beech, Lootable is a simple idea for a toilet paper holder that uses minimal material components.

01 Bronto children's chair
02 Lootable

INTERLOCKING SHAPES →

01

WHAT: Hexons
WHO: Pepper-mint
WHERE: United Kingdom
MATERIALS: Acrylic
QUALITIES: Multiple
creations from one form

Practical objects that are also fun
for the owner are what interests
London's Pepper-mint. Hexons are a
versatile set of interlocking shapes
that offer many possibilities to the
user. Exquisite chandeliers, table
lights, fruit bowls, and candelabras
can be formed by simply reconfiguring
a set of interlocking, translucent
pieces formed from one manufactured
shape. The idea is that this
interactive form of design will
encourage the latent designer to take
a more active role in shaping their
own personal space.

03

01 Large frost chandelier
   configuration
02 Large clear chandelier
   configuration
03 Small frost lampshade
04 Lampshades in clear and
   frost

SELF-ASSEMBLY SEATING →

68/69

WHAT: Chairfix
WHO: Ben Wilson with various artists
WHERE: United Kingdom
MATERIALS: Birch-faced plywood
QUALITIES: Minimal materials, "self packaging," no glue or adhesives, packs and ships flat

Ben Wilson's Chairfix series was inspired by self-assembly model airplane kits known as Airfix. Constructed from a single sheet of birch-faced plywood, this clever design uses a flat frame to cofunction as the package, making it lightweight and easily transportable. The individual pieces simply pop out of the frame and snap together without the need for glue or screws. For its launch Wilson invited a selection of artists to customize Chairfix. These were released as a limited-edition of 50 stools, in collaboration with Stussy.

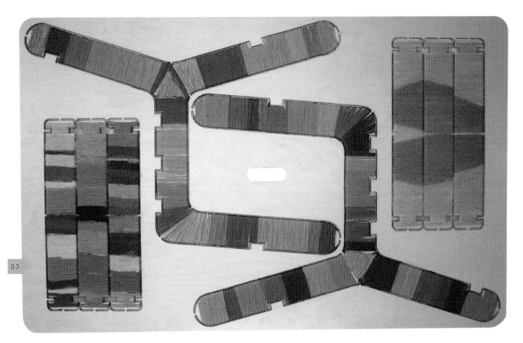

03

04

05

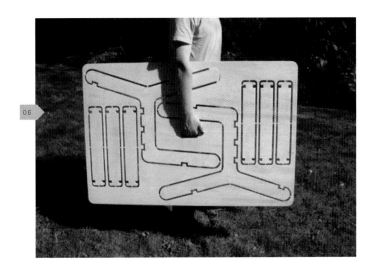

06

01 Chairfix, Oscar Wilson
02 Stussy Stool, Pete Fowler
03 Wooly Chair, Sarah Wilson
04 Wooly Chair, Sarah Wilson /
   Green Chair, Oscar Wilson
05 Sit On My Faces, Akt One
06 The self-assembly kit
   provides its own packaging,
   and is easy to carry

TRANSPORTABLE CHAIR →

01

WHAT: Box Up chair
WHO: Peter Hancheck
WHERE: United States
MATERIALS: Felt, plywood
QUALITIES: Transportable,
low-impact materials,
easy to assemble

A transient lifestyle brings the excitement of new locations, environments, and people, but often leads to restrictions on space and personal possessions, especially furniture. Box Up is Peter Hancheck's response to this lifestyle. While traveling during his university days, Hancheck often found himself coming home without a comfortable place to sit, so home never felt quite like home. His solution is Box Up, a soft, warm, friendly seat designed specifically for ease of transportation and assembly. With Box Up, the seat itself is the carrying case for its structural components. The pieces are put back together using snap fasteners. With its built-in handle, the chair is easy to transport even when assembled. Its honest construction, which displays the materials used, becomes a unique esthetic. Hancheck's choice of eco-friendly materials includes plywood and felt, which are both natural and biodegradable.

01 Kit of parts
02 Box up chair constructed

FLAT-PACK FURNITURE →

WHAT: PrefabDesign
furniture
WHO: Dave Keune
WHERE: The Netherlands
MATERIALS: Birch or maple
plywood
QUALITIES: Minimal
materials, packs flat, no
glue or adhesives

Dave Keune likes to think that the do-it-yourself quality of his PrefabDesign makes it people-friendly. This childrens' furniture set was designed for self-assembly by a parent and child, creating a meaningful and engaging, yet easy experience. His PrefabDesign encourages the buyer to be involved with the construction of the product which, for Keune, is in contradiction with current culture. By putting together the final object, the owner is more likely to develop an emotional bond with the product and to keep it for a long time. PrefabDesign also packs flat for ease of transport and minimal use of materials.

01 The PrefabDesign table is
   easy to transport
02 PrefabDesign table flatpack
03 PrefabDesign table assembled

The Neo Amish seat is available as a chair and a couch. Designed by Superhappybunny's Bart Haney, it is another example of flat-pack furniture with a pure minimalist approach to form and materials. The Neo Amish range is constructed from premium birch plywood and packs flat for shipping and storage. The pieces fit together without any fasteners or glue, and the seat is easy to assemble. Each comes complete with a "bunny banger mallet" for secure construction.

01 Neo Amish Seating side views
02 Neo Amish Seating front view

FLAT-PACK FURNITURE →

02

01

74/75

Modular furniture offers a people-friendly solution, as the manufacturer and the owner can assemble and disassemble. Flat pieces make it easy to ship and transport—a quality that saves space, time, and money for both the manufacturer and buyer. Erik Newman's Doveseat furniture collection is entirely handcrafted, packs flat, and is assembled without any adhesives.

Material choice is also a major consideration in his work. "For a period of time I couldn't bring myself to buy new wood, which tends to limit production." Newman designs with the strong conviction that the production of an object creates a demand for the material used. The materials he selects for his designs are always given great consideration: he believes that the materials selected should depend on their performance and environmental impact.

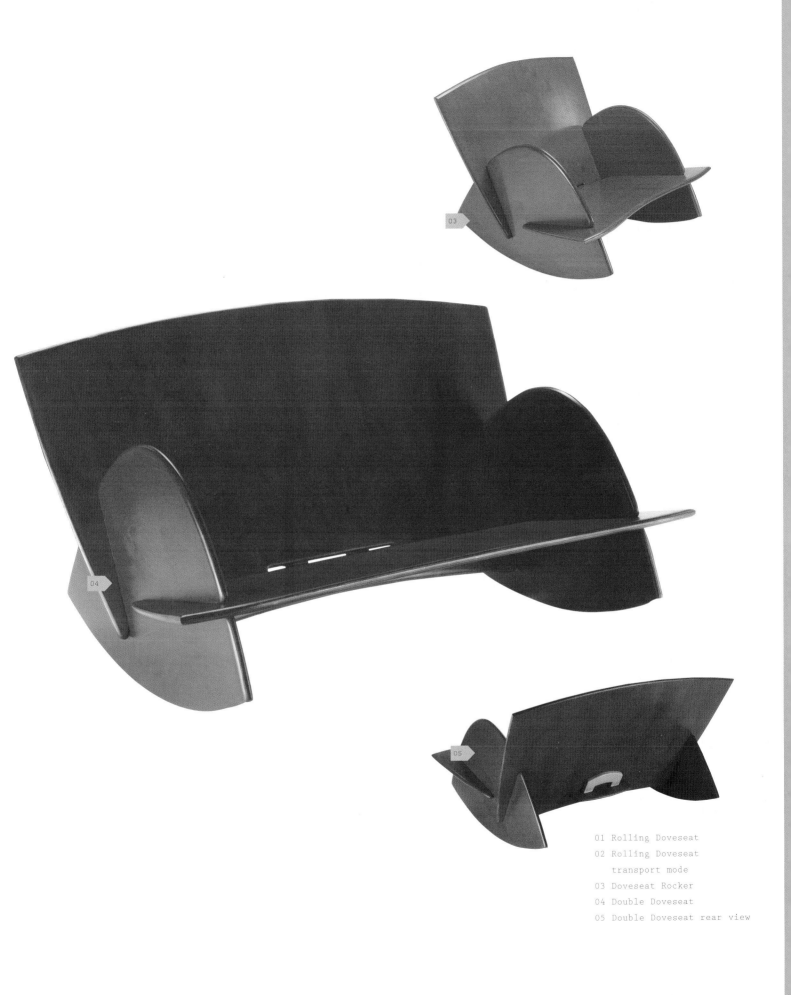

01 Rolling Doveseat
02 Rolling Doveseat
   transport mode
03 Doveseat Rocker
04 Double Doveseat
05 Double Doveseat rear view

CUSTOM KITCHENS →

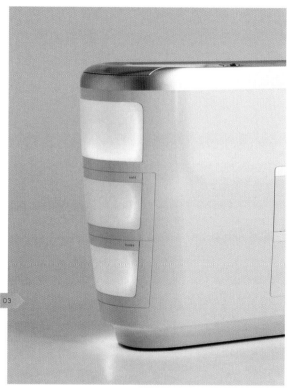

WHAT: In.Kitchen
WHO: Whirlpool
WHERE: International
MATERIALS: Various
QUALITIES: Modular
components, space
saving, energy efficient

Whirlpool sees consumers gravitating toward more meaningful and lasting products rather than luxury items. With its multifunctional, compact, and flexible design, In.Kitchen helps save space and time. Whirlpool has created a series of modular, space-saving kitchen components that allow a generous degree of custom configuration and adaptability for diverse and ever-changing lifestyles. Four concept kitchen configurations—Equipment, Theater, Ritual, and Built-Out—capitalize on different emotional and utilitarian aspects of cooking.

The essence of Ritual is basic in both function and emotion; it does not feature all the functionality of a traditional kitchen but rather a selection of what is perceived as the most necessary. There is no microwave, for instance, and special pans replace traditional oven cooking. Simplifying the traditional kitchen layout not only cuts down on unnecessary or unused appliances and devices, but also creates a more hands-on and emotional experience of cooking.

Equipment concentrates on the "efficient
cooking experience" and helps the user
cut down on the time and space
dedicated to food preparation and
consumption. This is done by paring down
the size, materials, form, and interface
of the kitchen and ensuring ease of
use. The entire work surface is smooth
and accessible, and makes maximum use
of space within tight constraints.
The dishwasher has a 3-minute dishwasher
program. From the outside, Equipment
appears to be an oversized freezer,
but its contents reveal a compact
and self-contained full kitchen unit.

01 Built-Out component
02 Theatre fittings
03 Ritual detail
04 Built-Out sink
05 Ritual detail

TEMPORARY HOUSING →

WHAT: Future Shack
WHO: Sean Godsell
Architects
WHERE: Australia
MATERIALS: Recycled
shipping containers,
plywood, various
QUALITIES: Modular
components, ease of
transit, self-
sustainable, humanitarian

Designed by Sean Godsell Architects, the Future Shack is a housing solution to humanitarian issues. Designed as emergency relief housing, Future Shack is formed from recycled shipping containers that are easily mass-produced, inexpensive, and easy to ship.

A completely self-contained unit, this design can be configured within 24 hours and is equipped with water tanks, solar-power cells, access ramps, a roof ladder, parasol roof, and support structure. A satellite receiver and external light bracket double as braces for the glass doors when in transit. After construction, Future Shack is completely self-sustainable, as it is capable of generating electricity. To complete the utilitarian kit, the interior is packed with tools for rehabilitation including clothing, food, and blankets. Future Shack promotes "good design" with a worldwide application for diverse needs—whether in post-disaster situations, temporary, or remote housing, or in the developing world.

01 Interior of Future Shack
02 Front view
03 Side view
04 Washroom
05 Living/dining area
06 (following page) Access ramp

01

02

Designframe, a design and product development consultancy, has produced the compact Pause stool, a light, collapsible stool composed entirely of recycled, corrugated cardboard, which is easy to fold up flat for storage. Constructed from one piece, the stool is lightweight, collapses to 1in (c. 2.5cm) for ease of transport and storage, and is inexpensive.

01 Pause stool, assembled
02 Assembly in progress

ENERGY-SAVING LIGHTING →

01

WHAT: Solar Bud, Pod
Lens, Star LED
WHO: Luceplan
WHERE: International
MATERIALS: Aluminum,
polycarbonate, metalized
methacrylate, LEDs,
rechargable batteries
QUALITIES: Energy
efficient

Luceplan's goal is to create interior and exterior lighting that enhances quality of life. Energy-saving features are a top priority and are considered at every step of the life cycle, from product manufacturing to durability and maintenance during use. Luceplan's own philosophy is to create long-lasting designs that are technologically sound and environmentally compatible as well as being beautiful objects that outlive fashion trends.

A few of Luceplan's energy efficient designs are the Solar Bud, Pod Lens, and Star LED. An outdoor lighting design, Solar Bud's battery is charged by sunlight, which allows it to provide ample lighting throughout the night (13 to 15 hours when fully charged). The Pod Lens can be suspended, stuck into the ground, or clustered in bunches to provide lighting for your garden, patio, or terrace. Reminiscent of flower buds, the Pod Lens is waterproof, UV-resistant, and takes both energy-saving and normal incandescent bulbs. The Star LED light is a modern interpretation of a candle that, with its rechargeable lights, can last for ever. The Star LED is small and light enough to take with you wherever you go.

01 Star LED
02 Solar Bud
03 Solar Bud
04 Pod Lens

FLAT-PACK FURNITURE →

84/85

<u>WHAT: 2-Way tables</u>
<u>WHO: Truck</u>
<u>WHERE: United States</u>
<u>MATERIALS: Permacore</u>
<u>QUALITIES: Minimal</u>
<u>materials, packs flat, no</u>
<u>glue or adhesives</u>

Truck's 2-Way table is so-named because it can be used in two ways; the modular top piece has a reversible design. The Tenon line was created with eco-friendly Permacore, a durable composite material made from 100-percent recovered and recycled wood fiber.

01 2-Way mini table
02 2-Way lounge in graphite
03 2-Way big lounge

01 Assembly of TRUCKids table
02 Assembly of TRUCKids chair

WHAT: TRUCKids furniture
WHO: Truck
WHERE: United States
MATERIALS: Baltic
plywood
QUALITIES: Minimal
materials, packs flat, no
glue or adhesives

TRUCKids furniture series allows
children to take charge of their
surroundings. The furniture, made of
Baltic plywood, packs flat for easy
shipping, transportation, and storage.
Child-friendly assembly stimulates
children to learn about construction
while having fun. The simple shapes
of the component pieces snap together
easily, free of adhesives. Corners
have been thoughtfully rounded for
safe use.

CUSTOM SPEAKERS →

01 Artcoustic speakers in situ
02 Artcoustic prints are available custom-made or decorated by contributing artists
03 Artcoustic blank screens

86/87

WHAT: Artcoustic speakers
WHO: Artcoustic
WHERE: Denmark
MATERIALS: Silk, cotton, steel
QUALITIES: Low-impact materials, modular components

Artcoustic solves the conflict between what looks good and what sounds good. Their state-of-the-art speakers, designed with a clean, timeless style, also double as a constantly changing art piece. Their appearance can be altered by the user, as the front screen of the speaker face is replaceable at any time. Artcoustic offers a variety of options for this front face, whether it be a solid color fabric, an artist's print, or your own personal artwork or photography. All of these fabric screens are made with natural materials such as silk or cotton. The inks used to print the imagery are all water based, completing the product's eco-friendly construction.

01

The vision of design duo Bless looks beyond the confined limits of art and fashion. Desiree Heiss and Ines Kaag create highly fashionable objects with a conceptual, human, functional, and often quirky twist. With their Design Relativators collection, Bless reinterprets the obtrusive design of unavoidable everyday objects. In an attempt to make necessary products more useful—and attractive—the designers chose to give items such as blenders, irons, and hairdryers a second function. Their reinvention of the vacuum cleaner transforms it into an attractive chair that houses a vacuum device within the seat. No longer do you have to watch the vacuum collect dust when not in use.

OTTOMAN FOOTSTOOLS →

88/89

WHAT: The Ottoman Project
WHO: Bart Bettencourt
with various artists
WHERE: United States
MATERIALS: Reclaimed
wood, recycled textiles
QUALITIES: Reclaimed
materials

The Ottoman Project is an ongoing collaboration between artists and designers to create one-of-a-kind art that you can sit on. The 24in (c. 60cm) diameter wooden bases, designed and constructed by Bart Bettencourt, are all created using reclaimed wood, while the cushions flaunt a clever and diverse use of found materials and fabrics.

Imaginative minds might use anything from old mattress tops to discarded museum upholstery. A diverse lineup of designers and street artists, including Rostarr, Futura, Colleen Rae Smiley, Kaws, and Heather Dunbar, give these ottomans their edgy style.

COMPACTIBLE OBJECTS →

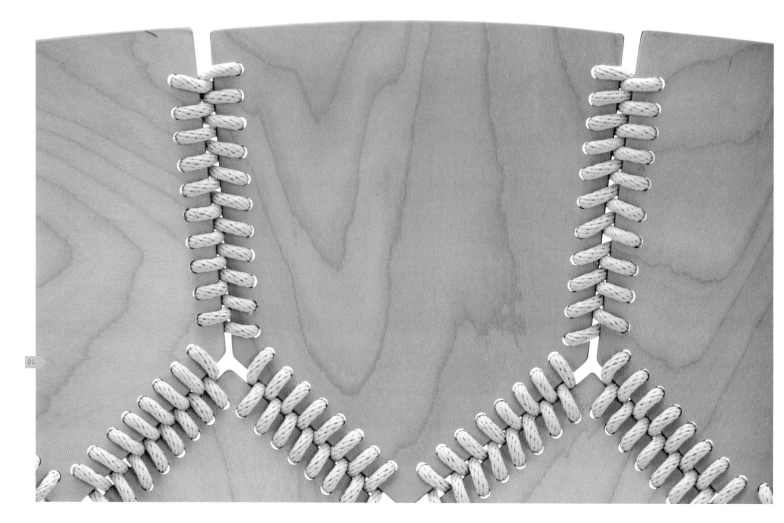

01

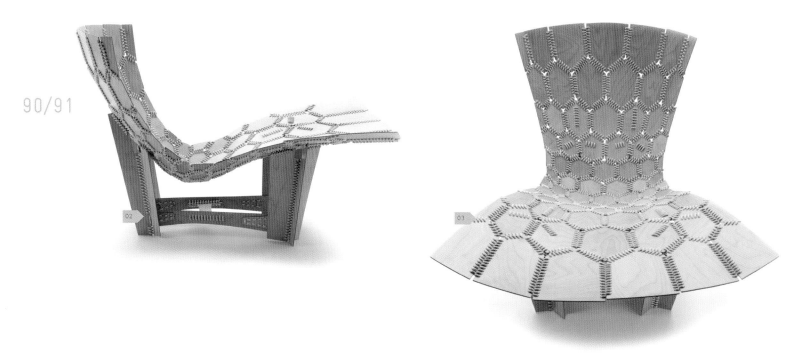

02

03

WHAT: Knit Chair
WHO: Emiliano Godoy
WHERE: United States,
Mexico
MATERIALS: Plywood,
cotton rope
QUALITIES: Natural,
biodegradable materials,
easy to transport,
modular components

Emiliano Godoy's Knit Chair and Beem
Trashcan (see following page) both
use biodegradable and compostible
materials. The Knit Chair is created
from small pieces of plywood and held
together with ordinary cotton rope.
Due to its construction, the Knit
Chair is naturally lightweight and
flexible, and adapts to the user's
body for comfortable seating.

01 Knit Chair detail
02 Side view
03 Front view
04 Side view
05 Front view

COMPACTIBLE OBJECTS →

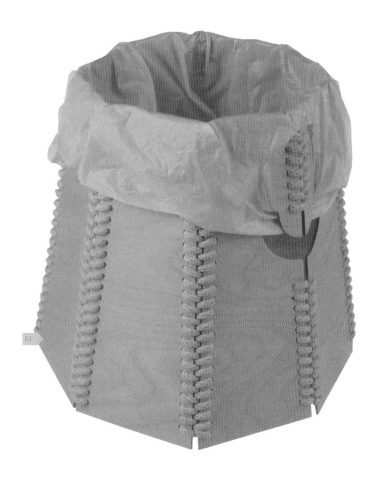

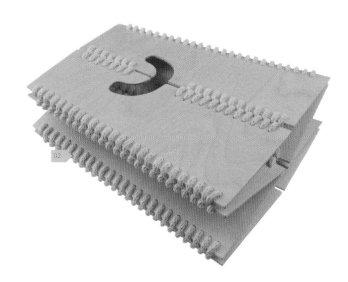

92/93

Like the Knit Chair, the Beem
Trashcan's plywood form is held
together with cotton rope. The rope
acts as the structural element as well
as a flexible connection, allowing the
trashcan to fold and collapse for easy
storage when not in use.

01 Beem Trashcan
02 Beem Trashcan collapsed

WHAT: Bamboo Furniture
Line
WHO: Peter Danko
WHERE: United States
MATERIALS: Bent plywood
QUALITIES: Efficiently
manufactured materials,
low-impact materials

Peter Danko, of Danko Persing, utilizes
the most eco-friendly materials and
manufacturing to produce affordable
furniture. His choice material—bent
plywood—yields a sturdy and sustainable
product; bent ply veneer harnesses
eight to ten times more usable wood
from a single log than solid lumber.
Danko finishes every work with
nontoxic, water-based adhesives,
and uses recycled materials for seat
suspension and padding. For Danko,
the key to becoming a sustainable
culture is to integrate eco-friendly
considerations into good design.

01 Cricked chair
02 Europa side chairs

MODULAR HOUSING →

94/95

WHAT: M-vironments
WHO: Michael Jantzen
WHERE: United States
MATERIALS: Steel, cement
with foam insulation
QUALITIES: Inter-
changeability, multiple
uses, recyclable
materials

Imagine a world in which structures can be created merely by combining a variety of modular components. Architect Michael Jantzen focuses his architectural efforts on merging conceptual ideas, art, design, and architecture into one experience. With M-vironments, relocatable structures are made from a wide variety of components that can be combined in many different ways to form a matrix of modular support frames. These frames can be assembled, in a variety of forms, and disassembled to accommodate changing needs. By capitalizing on the multiple uses of one basic shape, energy used during manufacturing processes and transportation can be reduced. Instead of having to recycle the materials, you can recycle the M-vironments by disassembling the components and then reassembling them to form different structures for different needs.

The M-house is created from this system. It consists of panels that are attached to an open-frame grid of interlocking cubes. Panels fold and unfold to create open platforms to shade the sun, deflect the rain, or block the wind, or to make spaces for work, play, sleeping, or eating. The house is designed to be self-sufficient, powered by sustainable energy sources such as wind and sun.

01 M-House exterior
02 M-House interior

WHAT: Growth Accelerator
WHO: Michael Jantzen
WHERE: United States
MATERIALS: Steel,polycarbonate plastic glazing
QUALITIES: Energy efficient

Designed as part of a series of greenhouses, the Growth Accelerator was developed to be as energy efficient as possible. The Growth Accelerator is a computer-controlled, super-efficient greenhouse, designed to grow plants at an accelerated rate. It provides the optimal interior environment in which plants will grow, yet only a small amount of energy is required for heating, cooling, ventilation, watering, and lighting as it is powered by solar energy.

The structure's shape forms a living space for plants and their human caretaker. On sunny days the plants stay out of the insulated chamber, where the solar energy collected charges the solar heating storage containers. At night and on cloudy days, the plants are automatically pulled into the insulated chamber, where the stored heat is used to keep them warm.

03

WHAT: Solar Residence
WHO: Michael Jantzen
WHERE: United States
MATERIALS: Steel, polycarbonate plastic glazing, foam
QUALITIES: Energy efficient

Jantzen's Solar Residence was an attempt to solve the problem of creating a low-cost house that was extremely energy efficient without the need for special tools or machinery. The Solar Residence is heavily insulated with foam, solar heated and cooled, and naturally ventilated. All of its appliances and lighting were chosen for their high energy efficiency.

01 Growth Accelerator
02 Solar Residence exterior
03 Solar Residence interior

PREFABRICATED BUILDINGS →

98/99

WHAT: Capsule House K
WHO: Kisho Kurokawa
Architect & Associates
WHERE: Japan
MATERIALS: Various
QUALITIES: Modular
components, harnesses
renewable energy,
sympathetic with
natural surroundings,
cost-effective

How do you create a modular house that will also suit the needs and tastes of its possible individual occupants? The architecture of Dr. Kisho Kurokawa experiments with this question and offers engaging solutions, such as the summer home Capsule House K.

Built into a steep hillside to complement the natural setting, this architectural structure is formed with an anchoring central base into which a series of prefabricated capsules can be placed to create a customized dwelling. Architecture that takes advantage of modular or prefabricated components is cost-effective in manufacturing and construction, as essentially only one type of component is produced.

Capsule House K also maximizes flexibility in order to meet the particular needs of its occupant.

The roof of Capsule House K is level
with the road, which allows the space
to double as a terrace or driveway,
and the exterior is maintenance-free,
complete with corrosion-resistant
steel. The home is almost self-reliant
in terms of energy use, with solar
panels to generate electricity, water
heating, and lighting. Water used by
its occupants can be recycled. Capsule
House K creates true harmony between
its man-made and natural surroundings.

01 Interior of Capsule House K
02 The roof terraces
03 The hillside setting
04 Projecting side windows

03—

IMAGINATIVE REUSE

Bart Bettencourt and Carlos Salgado / Colleen Rae Smiley / Manuel Wijffels / URoads / nydesignroom / Eva Menz / Demano / Sonic Design / Carrie Collins / Co-lab

Selecting recycled materials is the ideal choice for designers, but manufacturing recycled materials still takes time and energy. So why not recycle by using found materials? The designers in the following section have all skipped much of the manufacturing process by reclaiming discarded materials that they have found around them. Sparkling chandeliers are assembled from pieces of clear plastic soda bottles, clever lighting is formed from soup cans, modern furniture is built from woodshop scraps, and one-of-a-kind quilts are stiched from discarded scraps. These are just a few of the designers who have opened up their eyes to the possibilities of reusing materials.

DESIGNING TIME
ED VAN HINTE

Going to Mars doesn't really get you anywhere. However, it takes a huge effort, in terms of time, money, and danger, and for some reason we humans seem to like that. We're always so damn industrious. In fact we all seem to suffer from Attention Deficit Hyperactivity Disorder, and the results are usually questionable, to put it mildly. We try to recreate ourselves in God's image, but end up being a bunch of clumsy troublemakers. The wisdom that a better option might be to do nothing has almost completely evaporated from our minds, even although it is the tacit idea behind all technological development: free us from productive activities to idly enjoy the blessings of full-blown automation. It is absolutely weird that, instead, designers and engineers are constantly busy, deadline after deadline, developing things, commodities, that are either meant for saving time, like airplanes, washing machines, and robots, or for wasting time, like weapons, video games, and even more robots. Cars provide us with speed, convenience, and comfort, while training bikes make us sweat to stay fit, but without the benefit of moving from one place to another. They are the uppers and downers of our lives, not necessarily in any specific order. My father was a psychiatrist in a hospital. Whenever he took in a new patient for his ward, the first thing he did was stop all medicine, sometimes as much as an ounce of pills. More often than not the patient's condition immediately improved because of that. Maybe that is what we ought to do: stop creating all these silly life-improving gizmos, at least for a while, just to see what happens.

CONSERVING EFFORT
This does not imply that design would have to disappear altogether. Presupposing that the system to provide the world population with water, food, and shelter would be in a state of perfection (which is not likely to ever happen) the difference would be that design would no longer be concerned with new objects. A modest start has already been made with reduction of the number of material creations. Some designers actually succeed in making a living by avoiding designing new objects, resulting in reduced use of materials and reduced pollution. One of those is an architect—Willem Jan Neutelings. He is an advocate of professional laziness. In the late 1990s he was requested to design an appartment building to replace an old manor house that was due to be demolished. He decided not to do that, but to have it restored instead, complete with a garden, and build a smaller modern block right next to it. The response was rather surprising; people started complaining that the architect had designed an ugly modern block right next to a lovely romantic house. They didn't know that if it weren't for Neutelings, it simply wouldn't have survived.

Given the opportunity, designer Jan Konings is even more radical. Some years ago the Dutch Society for Nature Monuments assigned him, via the Netherlands Design Institute, to develop ideas for ways in which this large nature conservation organization could present itself to the public. His propositions were minimal. He suggested that trees could be chopped down and shredded, and that the remains could be used to flatten out parking areas on the spot where the trees used to be. Another plan of his was to stick pieces of paper to trees with "WC" on them, to point out where visitors of nature answer its call. Later he was assigned to design a reception desk for the Dutch pavilion at the

World Expo in Hannover, Germany. His proposition was—you must have guessed it—not to make a desk at all, but instead to provide the pavilion's personnel with mobile communication equipment so that every employee, walking freely around in the building, would have access to all the information needed to help visitors. His solution was not accepted, which in this case meant that part of it—no desk—still became a success.

RECLAIMING FREE TIME

Not to design objects is of course only part of the solution in reaching Lazytopia, the land of doing next to nothing, or as Dutch poet Remco Campert put it "nothing, but what would add up to the same anyway." The rest of us are left with adrenaline, time, and no commodities to take it from us. Therefore, design needs to change its focus from objects to scenarios and simple means to help us waste time in harmless ways, without feeling guilty about failed commitments. A rudiment of this kind of pastime still exists. It is not necessarily to be experienced on weekends or during holidays. It is not to be found in specially designed leisure accomodations. No, it is the extra hours or even minutes of spare time you get when something goes wrong in your action flow. You have missed a plane, have to wait for someone or something to turn up, or better still, someone has cancelled an appointment with you. You have time on your hands and you're not to blame. That overrules any feelings of guilt. That is the kind of time in which truly harmless activities are invented: feed the birds, take a walk, sit on a fallen tree, and watch other people.

For that kind of time designers could start to develop scenarios for lazy behavior. It could consist of ingenious sequences of engaging play, preferably without the need for any tools, certainly not the kind that need energy. The secret is in finding ways to let humans waste time with almost nothing—earth, stones, pieces of wood. It would be best if everyone did all this alone, not necessarily without company, but without commitments and appointments, because they are the beginning of efficiency and the notion of time. Because that is what I'm talking about: designing time in such a way that it goes by unnoticed. People could write and draw in the sand, think, dig holes, build castles, make sounds and listen to them. When people are together, accidentally of course, they can play games, dance, or compete. They would do minimum damage to their own biotope. They could also make their own equipment, build towers, invent ways to empower themselves, and who knows, maybe even construct wind-powered vehicles.

RECLAIMED-WOOD FURNITURE →

01

WHAT: Scrapile
WHO: Bart Bettencourt and
Carlos Salgado
WHERE: United States
MATERIALS: Reclaimed wood
QUALITIES: Reclaimed
materials, nontoxic
materials

Scrapile, a collaborative project between designers Bart Bettencourt and Carlos Salgado, uses discarded bits of wood to create unique furniture pieces. A wide range of wood varieties—including poplar, walnut, bamboo, plywood, yellow pine, and cherry—are laminated using nontoxic, water-soluble glue.

The end results are minimalist benches, tables, and shelving with a unique esthetic. Scrapile wood is all 100-percent reclaimed. The raw material comes from an array of sources including local woodworking studios, Bettencourt and Salgado's own studios, and even the occasional piano manufacturer. The concept that inspires Scrapile is the notion that these discarded materials are reintroduced as functional objects instead of filling up local landfills.

02

03

01 Mod shelves
02 Small solid bench
03 Hex stool

RECLAIMED-FABRIC QUILTS →

01

106/107

WHAT: Quilts
WHO: Colleen Rae Smiley
WHERE: United States
MATERIALS: Reclaimed
textiles
QUALITIES: Reclaimed
materials

The very nature of a quilt is to tell a story—the story of a family's past or even a nation or culture's heritage. Each of the reclaimed fabrics in Colleen Smiley's quilts has its own history to tell. Pieces for her patchwork may come from discarded upholstery from museums, including the Guggenheim, unused fabric from friends, flea markets, vintage coats, or even unwanted couches. These layers add a history and narrative to the pieces, which become objects of both art and comfort. Each quilt is unique and entirely handmade by Smiley. Her Beach Quilt was formed from nylon flag material and boy scout kerchief seconds, unusable because of printing mistakes. Snaps and attachable plastic spikes were added for comfortable and functional use during picnics or beach outings.

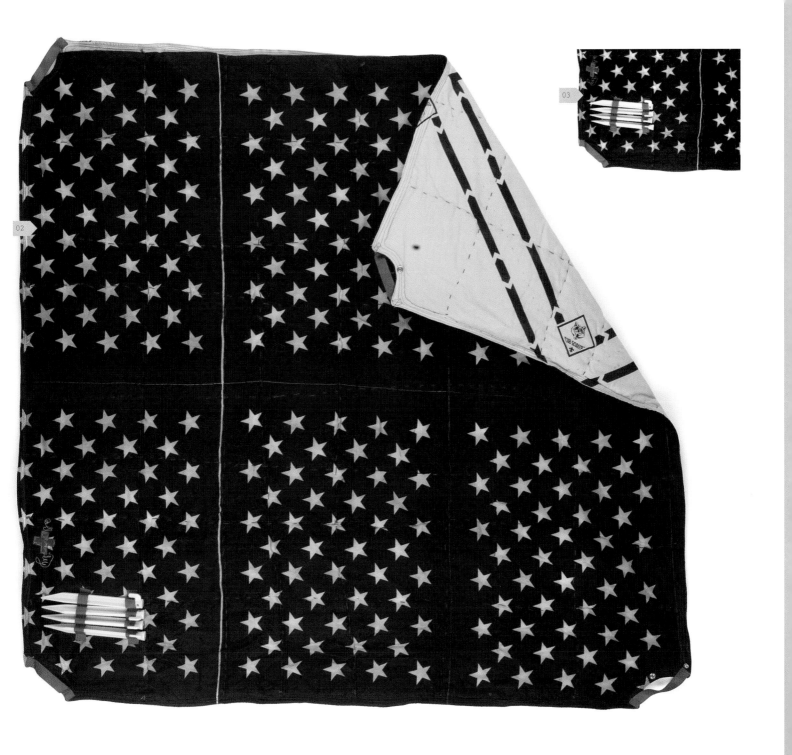

01 Pillow
02 Flag-and-boy-scout-kerchief
   beach blanket
03 Detail of beach blanket

04

05

06

07

04-07 A selection of quilt
designs

<u>RECYCLED</u> <u>FASHION</u> →

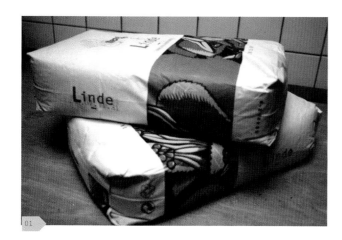

<u>WHAT: BackPaper</u>
<u>WHO: Manuel Wijffels</u>
<u>WHERE: The Netherlands</u>
<u>MATERIALS: Flour bags</u>
<u>QUALITIES: Reclaimed,</u>
<u>recycled materials</u>

Dutch designer Manuel Wijffels finds unique and clever ways to reuse simple, everyday products that tend to be overlooked. BackPaper was created by simply adding a single element—the shoulder straps—to an already visually attractive flour bag. The result is a fashionable, ready-to-wear carryall. Although the bags are made from paper, they are quite strong and resilient.

01 Flour bag
02 Flour-bag backpack

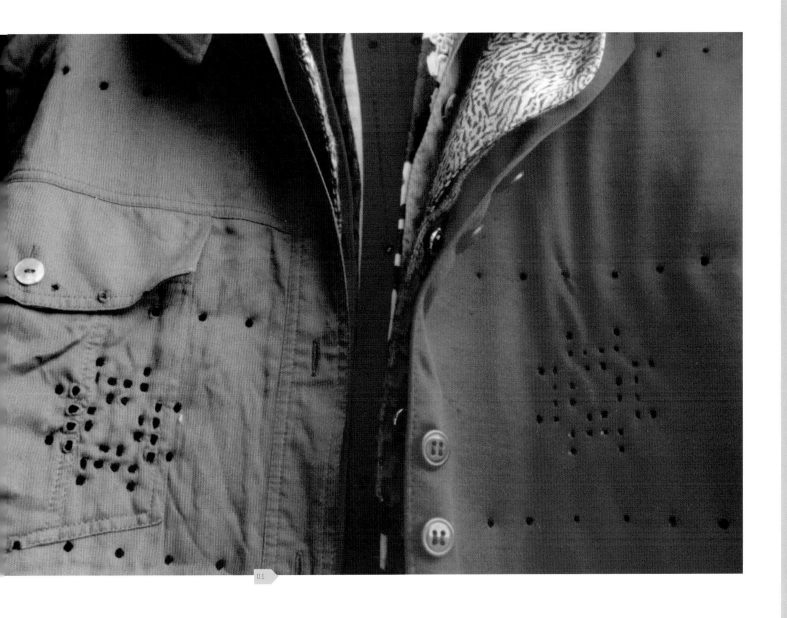

01

01 Jacket detail

From Rags to Riches, from Riches to
Rhyme is another resourceful Wijffels
concept. With the realization that more
and more recycled textiles will be
synthetic, the goal was to capitalize
on a dominant characteristic: it melts
when heated. Synthetic shirts were
selected from a textile recycling
center and heated using a hot needle

process; this fuses the layers and at
the same time creates patterns. For
the best effect, the textile was
pressed in between two perforated metal
sheets, which helped orient and melt
the patterns together. The result is
distinctive, fresh solutions from
common discard.

RECYCLED-RUBBER SOLES →

01

112/113

WHAT: Recycled shoes
WHO: URoads
WHERE: Italy
MATERIALS: Reclaimed
tire treads
QUALITIES: Recycled
materials

Fashion is often obsessed with what is new and tends to ignore its effects on the environment. However, footwear brand URoads (which stands for Your Roads thus Our Roads) has created a new way to make discarded tires useful again with the utmost practicality and style. Adding to the value of the product, each pair of URoads is handcrafted, with careful attention paid to detail. This guarantees that no two pairs are alike. In addition to using recycled treads, URoads utilizes recycled papers, and other materials that reduce environmental impact. Accompanying materials complement the URoads philosophy—they include cool, natural linens, tanned leathers, and rustic, worn accessories—and the shoes are handstitched and handfinished.

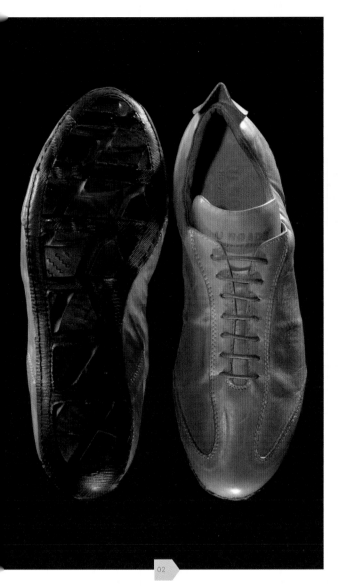

01 Off-road collection
02 Recycled tire sole
03 URoad boot

RECONSTRUCTED GARMENTS →

WHAT: Trash-à-Porter
WHO: nydesignroom
WHERE: United States
MATERIALS: Reclaimed
textiles
QUALITIES: Recycled
materials

Reconstructing fashion for men and women, Trash-à-Porter is the in-house eco-friendly clothing line by nydesignroom. For Ggrippo, designer of Trash-à-Porter, "clothes from fashion eras long gone are the perfect medium from which to form a vivid new line of fashionable tees and beautiful dresses." Midsections from one garment and crewnecks from another are fused into a reconstructed new item. Pieces are collected from various places. For instance, cashmere and T-shirts might come from a secondhand wholesaler, and suits from a local, little-known thrift shop. Sometimes pieces from past collections are revived to become new again in another line. Most of Trash-à-Porter's creations are created in nydesignroom's Brooklyn studio, individually designed and put together as unique one-offs. Inspired by the urban street culture of New York and its multicultural surroundings, Trash-à-Porter's collections are vibrant interpretations of fashion's obsession with vintage clothing.

"In a civilization that pushes
for overproduction and mass
consumption, Trash-à-Porter takes
a step back and redefines the
art of reinventing."

01 The 1999 collection was the
   work of artist Brancusi
02 The 2001 collection was
   inspired by a walk through
   New York City
03 Patch cashmere
04 Denim and cashmere

FOUND-OBJECT CHANDELIERS →

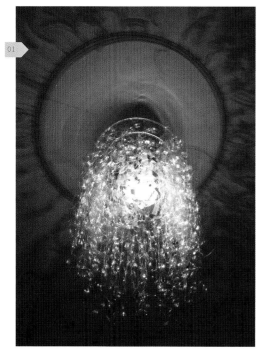

116/117

WHAT: Life Is Beautiful
collection
WHO: Eva Menz
WHERE: United Kingdom
MATERIALS: Clear plastic
soda bottles, found
objects, reclaimed
silk paper
QUALITIES: Recycled
materials

Eva Menz's chandelier collection "Life is Beautiful" aims to portray the beauty of the simple and often disregarded small details of life. Her chandeliers, traditionally seen as objects of glamor, are designed from not-so-glamorous materials. Her aim is to find leftover pieces from a domestic environment and assemble them into a pleasing sculptural arrangement. Entitled "Money Can't Buy Me Love," the chandelier above is

handmade from 100 clear plastic bottles. These were cut into pieces, joined together with a selection of found objects, and suspended with string. A selection of unwanted objects come together to form a truly glamorous chandelier.

Silk paper is often used to wrap something precious and fragile. Rather than simply wrapping another object, this material has become something

04

precious and fragile itself. For
1,000 Cranes, Menz took the used paper
wrapping from a light and folded it
into 1,000 paper cranes to create
another lighting piece. An ancient
paper-folding tradition holds that
a wish will come true for the person
who manages to fold 1,000 cranes.

RECYCLED BAGS →

01

118/119

WHAT: Bags
WHO: Demano
WHERE: Spain
MATERIALS: Discarded
event banners
QUALITY: Recycled
materials

Chances are, you've probably never wondered what will happen to those colorful city banners announcing the next festival or event. And who would think you'd be carrying it on your shoulder shortly after it's been discarded. One-of-a-kind Demano bags are crafted from the abundant event banners used to announce the various exhibitions, festivals, and cultural events that take place throughout

Barcelona. In collaboration with the city's cultural and civic institutions, Demano studies each banner and makes a point to keep and even strengthen its original message. In using a nonrecyclable material (PVC), Demano's bags have both an economic and an ecological impact. The diverse designs ensure the optimal use of each banner, to keep waste to an absolute minimum.

01 Marbella bag
02 Carmen bag
03 Ciutadella bag
04 Demano portafolio
05 Barceloneta bag

<u>REAPPROPRIATED</u> <u>OBJECTS</u> →

120/121

Klaus Rosburg spent a lot of his childhood making miniature boats and planes out of scrap metal and wood from his father's workshop. By the age of 12, having been the proud builder of several tree houses, rafts, a cabin with a home security system, and a customized tandem, Klaus knew he was on the path to industrial design; he later formed the studio Sonic Design.

Hangerlight, Deolight, and Condom Vase are playful and creative adaptations of everyday familiar objects. With Hangerlight, the simple, clear plastic hanger finds new life as the star of a unique lighting fixture. Twenty-five plastic hangers, mass-produced and available in 99-cent stores (Pound shops), are rotated around a bulb to create a new lighting fixture.

The Deolight flashlight was fabricated from a clear, recycled deodorant dispenser. Reusing the disposable housing and turning it into a new and fully functional product questions the need for designing increasingly complex and sophisticated structures for one-time use.

WHAT: Hangerlight
WHO: Sonic Design
WHERE: United States
MATERIALS: Clear plastic hangers
QUALITIES: Recycled materials

RECLAIMED-MATERIALS APPAREL →

01

122/123

WHAT: Fabric Horse
WHO: Carrie Collins
WHERE: United States
MATERIALS: Reclaimed
textiles
QUALITIES: Innovative
use of waste materials

Fabric Horse was created by Carrie Collins. With her interest in reusing durable materials in different ways she realizes that just about anything can become fabric. The functionality in the design makes these products strong, and with the utilization of unexpected fabrics they present a fresh style as well.

Fabric Horse uses any materials that can be stitched together. All the products are created from found materials, and each product is designed and handmade as a one-off.

As well as offering products, Fabric Horse offers custom design, stitching, and fabrication services.

The materials used here are from various sources, including used carpets, raincoats, clothing, belt buckles, old banners and signs, innertube covers, car-seat upholstery, seatbelts and buckles, and leftover vinyl woodgrain flooring from the designer's own bathroom.

01 Tan circle bag and wallet
02 Black utility belt
03 Blue circle bag
04 Decorative backpack
05 Lips bag

(photography: Melissa Enders;
styling: Elsa B. Shadley)

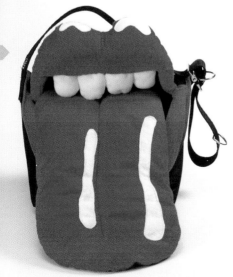

TREE STOOL →

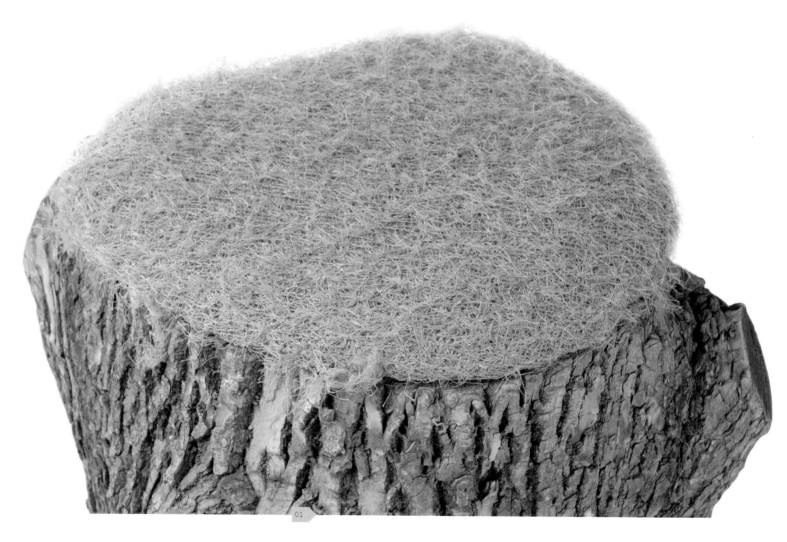

01

124/125

WHAT: Mossy Stub
WHO: Co-lab
WHERE: United States
MATERIALS: Tree stump,
reclaimed textiles
QUALITIES: Reclaimed
materials

Located in Detroit, Michigan, Co-lab is a creative team that aims to increase social-awareness of the environment through art, architecture, and design. To this end it has created a line of unique and clever products that are good for both people and the environment. Through these products it has created an inner-city enterprise that makes useful and beautiful products from salvaged, reused, recycled, or natural materials. The business, based in Detroit, employs local residents and "at risk" people who are typically underemployed, underpaid, or otherwise forced to commute long distances for minimum-wage jobs.

The Mossy Stub (pronounced "stoob," which means stump in Danish) is one of these products. Tree removal services often cut their trees into sections that make perfect stools. This stool, made from just such a section, has been upholstered with a very mossy looking fabric; the inside is padded with reclaimed stuffing.

02

01 Detail of upholstery fabric
02 Mossy Stub

04—

SOCIAL SENSIBILITY

Venture Snowboards / Patrik Fredriksons / Method / mop / Office of Mobile Design / Brooklyn Brewery / American Apparel / Patricia Johanson / Tsui Design & Research Inc. / Rinzen and Weiden+Kennedy / John Nicholson and Kathy Takayama / Fulguro and Thomas Jomini Architecture Studio/ Rob Thompson / SoftAir

Using eco-friendly materials and processes is just part of the solution to creating a more environment-conscious society. Making these products and their message available to the everyday consumer is another vital part of the equation. If being eco-conscious is to be an automatic part of the design process, then it should also be a part of the consumer's selection, which means creating products that are affordable, desirable, and fashionable. SoftAir is one of the companies that design specifically with young people in mind—with the youth pushing design and trends, accessiblity, function, and style are the uppermost priorities. Another part of the solution is to use the most responsible manufacturing processes, which harm neither people nor the environment. American Apparel is one company that has a "sweatshop free" philosophy; it creates stylish clothing without exploiting its labor force. Patricia Johanson creates park designs that benefit the natural habitat as well as the public. These companies and designers are part of a new movement to create products with social sensibility in mind.

LESS IS MORE FOR MANY MORE
JAN DRANGER

In 1961 I found a small article on page 29 in the daily newspaper saying that the world was heading toward a catastrophe at the end of the century. There would be starvation and pollution. Important materials would become scarce because of overconsumption, due to an explosion of population that had already started. If this were true, it would of course be the biggest thing that ever happened to the human race. So why was it on page 29? I obtained permission to take half a year off school to collect all the facts known by the UN and other institutions at the time. I concluded that even if the worst scenario didn't occur, this question would greatly affect the world in many ways: economically, socially, and politically. It was obvious there wasn't one miracle cure to fix it, but rather a myriad of large and small actions—everyone needed to contribute in their own way.

On a large scale, of course, there wasn't much I could do, yet it was possible for me to do something in the area I planned to work in: architecture or design.

DESIGN FOR THE PEOPLE
In the fields of art and design you have to find your own style or theme, to make your own mark. And in one small article I found such a theme, "less is more," from the functionalism of 1930s Bauhaus, but for a new reason and in a new context—more for less to many more.

Architects have always been engaged and paid by the establishment—by pharaohs, the church, by warlords and kings—often with an open-ended budget. Because of this, architecture grew increasingly sophisticated, exclusive, and remote from the people.

In 1965 everyday things were either well designed and expensive or, like the vast majority of products, cheap in every aspect. But you don't have to be rich to appreciate design. As a designer I was convinced things didn't need to be expensive to be adequately designed, especially if you could use innovation to reduce materials and cut the costs of distribution and stock, for example, by delivering flat-packed goods. By these means, many more products could be produced from the same quantity of material.

AFFORDABLE DESIGN
Instead of engaging in evermore sophisticated designs for those willing to pay, I decided to work with the basics. This would mean always considering a large volume of production, and export to larger populations than Sweden's. So from that short article and with all this in mind, in 1968 I went straight from design school, along with Johan Huldt, to set up a design studio called Innovator. Five years later Innovator was present in all continents and was also a major supplier to IKEA.

Innovator was based upon what today is called environment-adapted design: for example, we used a minimum of materials and made use of scrap materials and flat-pack construction. In this way, it was possible to bring prices down substantially. Much of our success came from the notion that this was the first collection of stylish furniture that was aimed at young people, just like the Beatles or blue jeans.

ENVIRONMENTAL AWARENESS

At that time the question of the environment was not high on the public agenda, unlike today, when a new project can't be launched without being thoroughly investigated from an ecological point of view. But we knew that in the years to come many people would be highly educated without necessarily having a lot of money to spend. This is also the reason why consumers are often ahead of producers, not least in ecological matters. This, however, does not mean they are willing to spend more for eco-products. And they shouldn't have to—eco is efficient and moneysaving.

Design involves making choices. One way of doing this is to write a demand specification of everything you want the product to achieve and then keep working until you can tick off each point. Eco-design means doubling or quadrupling the number of points on the list, but it is an interesting challenge that can lead to new solutions and design qualities—as well as proving an economic option.

Thirty years ago "industrial design" was rather unknown as a profession. Only at the end of the last century did design become established in industry in general. There has been an exponential increase in the number of designed products. At a time when there is no such thing as national design, when design really is universal, when all trends coexist at the same time and everything is possible, it is even more important that design have a purpose.

With millions of designs on the market, there has got to be a good reason to squeeze in another one. Eco-design is a very good reason, not only because of socioeconomic realities, but also because of a change in value systems that has started with the younger generations. They know that there is only one planet, though few would pay anything extra to save it.

CHANGING VALUES

Sixty years ago furniture was the family's second-biggest investment, after the house or apartment itself. Of course, this affected people's relationship to products. Many of my childhood friends were not allowed to enter some rooms in their home because their parents thought they would damage the furniture. These rooms were reserved for the few hours when guests were invited. Since the furniture was little used, it could be inherited, whether or not it was suitable for the next generation. Less expensive furniture allows people to realize that there are more important things in life than furniture, such as children.

Wave after wave of new technology has gradually eaten up the disposable income previously spent on furniture. First the radio, then the telephone, the car, the stereo, the TV, the computer, ski trips, and mobile phones. Less and less money is available for furniture. That's why furniture has become (and should be) less and less expensive.

Yet in the information age we are more aware about the quality of products and we demand that safety, hygiene, maintenance, and other considerations are built into our products, further emphasizing the need for more efficient products and production systems.

Throughout the years I have tried all kinds of materials, from paper to peanuts. Air has turned out to be the most efficient. SoftAir® (an inflatable furniture line available through IKEA) is a product of the information society. From hardware to software, and a less materialistic attitude to what life is all about.

SUSTAINABLE SNOWBOARDS →

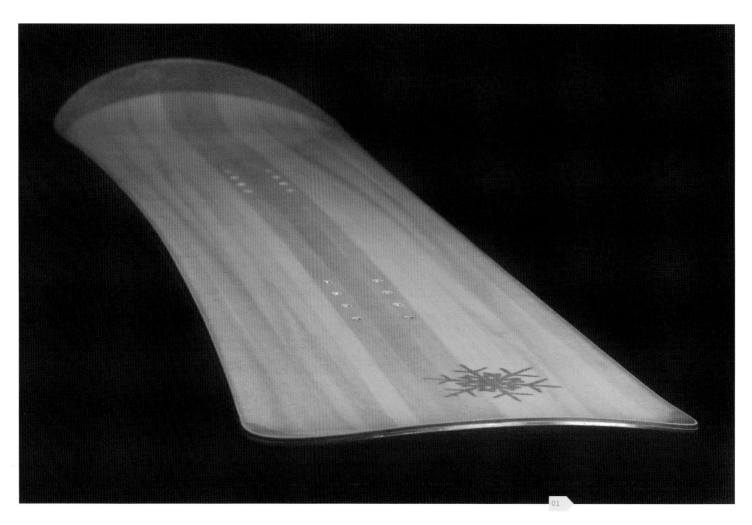

01

130/131

WHAT: Snowboards
WHO: Venture Snowboards
WHERE: United States
MATERIALS: Certified
wood, organic cotton
and hemp
QUALITIES: Sustainable
materials, alternative
energy used in
manufacture

Founded in 1999 by husband-and-wife team Klemens and Lisa Branner, Venture Snowboards is a small, independently owned snowboard manufacturer. Venture places equal emphasis on performance and environmental sustainability. The company builds all of its boards from scratch, using only Forest Stewardship Council certified wood to handcraft its signature bookmatched cores, and organic cotton and hemp fabrics for its topsheets. Normally, a variety of woods, plastics, fiberglass, and synthetic chemicals and materials are used in the construction of snowboards, which is not exactly eco-friendly. In addition to using quality natural materials, the Venture workshop is powered with energy harvested from wind power—a first in the snowboard industry. With simplicity as one of the company's key design principles, Venture has foregone typical snowboard graphics in favor of a clean, clear look. The end result is a product that is visually stunning, environmentally conscious, and technically superior.

01 Certified-wood board
02 Jason Brooks at Red Mountain
   (*photograph Ben Eng*)

RAW-WOOD TABLES →

01

WHAT: Table #1, Table #2
WHO: Patrik Fredriksons
WHERE: United Kingdom
MATERIALS: Certified
silver birch, steel
QUALITIES: Sustainable
materials, simplicity
of construction

Expressive and poetic, Patrik Fredriksons designs with a curious, unconventional, and enchanting sensibility. Formed from raw chunks of untreated birch, Table #1 and Table #2 form elegant, unconventional furniture pieces. The silver birch is native to the UK, and all the wood used comes from locally managed forests. The life span of this tree is relatively short, as a result of various fungal diseases. Removing the older trees quickly encourages regeneration, which benefits the wide variety of insects that rely on the silver birch.

Normally, most of the wood removed is burned, a process that releases harmful carbon dioxide into the atmosphere. Finding a second life for these logs by creating furniture is an eco-friendly solution.

ORGANIC TOILETRIES →

01

02

01 Magnolia dish soap
02 All-purpose cleaner

WHAT: Cleaning fluids
WHO: Method
WHERE: United States
MATERIALS: Certified
organic fruits,
vegetables, and herbs,
recyclable plastics
QUALITIES: Organic,
all-natural ingredients;
minimal, recyclable
packaging

Method has developed a line of cleaning solutions for surfaces, dishes, laundry, hands, and air. Their philosophy is to rid the world of dirt, and by "dirt" they mean the poisonous chemicals that pollute our water and air. All Method formulas contain only biodegradable ingredients, derived from natural materials such as soy, coconut, and palm oils. Their products are contained in minimal packaging made from the most recyclable plastics. Neither Method nor the suppliers of their raw materials use animal testing. Designed with wide accessibility in mind, Method products are readily available at major retailers, bringing natural cleaning products out of small health-food shops and into the mass market.

01-03 c-system products

The American National Standards Institute assures consumers that "certified organic ingredients" have no toxic and persistent pesticides, antibiotics, sewage sludge, irradiation, or genetically modified ingredients used in any phase of production, from farm to retail. Naturally, growing organically keeps our soil and water healthy and clean.

mop (modern organic products) is one company that meets these strict standards with pride, creating an affordable and accessible line of all-natural body and hair products from certified organic fruits, vegetables, and herbs. The light fragrances of mop products are the natural result of their pure ingredients.

ADAPTABLE MOBILE HOMES →

01

WHAT: Portable House
WHO: Office of Mobile Design
WHERE: United States
MATERIALS: Steel,
SIPS (structurally insulated
panel system), Polygal,
Homasote, BIOFIBER, Plyboo,
Expanko cork, tankless water
heater, passive cooling systems
QUALITIES: Environmentally
friendly architecture,
social awareness

The security, comfort, and pride of owning your own home is a universal desire and dream. However, as Jennifer Siegal has realized, this dream is often compromised. The Office of Mobile Design, headed by Siegal, works to reinterpret the negative connotations of the mobile home by creating lightweight, portable, practical, and affordable dwellings for all, with environmental responsibility a constant consideration.

The Portable House adapts, relocates, and reorients itself to accommodate an ever-changing environment. It offers an eco-sensitive and economical alternative to the increasingly expensive permanent structures that constitute most of today's housing options. At the same time, the Portable House calls into question preconceived notions of the trailer home and trailer park, creating an entirely new option for those with disposable income, but insufficient resources to own their own home.

The Portable House's expandable/
contractible spaces, varying degrees
of translucency, and its very
portability, render it uniquely
flexible and adaptable. Its central
kitchen/bath core divides and
separates the sleeping space from
the eating/living space in a compact
assemblage of form and function. When
additional space is required, the
living room structure can be extended
to increase square footage. By design,
the House can be maneuvered and
reoriented to take advantage of
natural light and airflow.

01 One of the possible Portable
   House orientations
02 Options for expansion

01

WHAT: Ecoville
WHO: Office of Mobile Design
WHERE: United States
MATERIALS: Steel, SIPS
(structurally insulated panel
system), Polygal, Homasote,
BIOFIBER, Plyboo, Expanko cork,
tankless water heater, passive
cooling systems
QUALITIES: Environmentally
friendly architecture,
social awareness

Transforming a 2$^{1}/_{2}$-acre (c. 1-hectare) lot in downtown Los Angeles into a sustainable artist-in-residence live/work community is the focus of the Ecoville project. The objective is to construct around 40 Portable House units, with an emphasis on native Californian, drought-resistant plant materials, common gardens, and the use of sustainable building materials. The development comprises a series of attached and semiattached buildings in multiple, stacked configurations. In an effort to provide affordable artists' residences, the development demonstrates that modern, individual design solutions are possible with mass-customization.

01

WHAT: Eco Lab
WHO: Office of Mobile Design
WHERE: United States
MATERIALS: Steel, SIPS
(structurally insulated panel
system), Polygal, Homasote,
BIOFIBER, Plyboo, Expanko cork,
tankless water heater, passive
cooling systems
QUALITIES: Environmentally
friendly architecture and
social awareness

The mobile Eco Lab was built in
collaboration with the Hollywood
Beautification Team, whose mission
is to restore beauty and integrity to
the Hollywood community. The 8 x 35ft
(c. $2^1/_2$ x $10^1/_2$m) trailer now travels
throughout Los Angeles County to
inform school children about the
importance of saving and protecting

the environment. As a working mobile
classroom, the Eco Lab provides a base
for a range of exhibitions, all of
which focus on ecology. Upon arrival
at the schoolyard, elevated walkways
fold down and slide out of the
trailer's body. The Eco Lab is
immediately recognizable as a place
for interaction, discovery, and fun.

02

ALTERNATIVE ENERGY →

01

142/143

WHAT: Beers and ales
WHO: Brooklyn Brewery
WHERE: United States
MATERIALS: Malt, hops,
water, glass
QUALITIES: Alternative
energy used in
manufacture, eco-friendly
disposal of waste, social
awareness

The Brooklyn Brewery creates beer with 100-percent alternative energy—wind power generated through windmills in upstate New York. In the spring of 2002, Brooklyn Brewery were contacted about switching over to alternative energy use. A few months later, the New York City blackout, an event that showed how extreme the city's energy use had become, sealed their decision. Moments afterward, the Brooklyn Brewery flipped the switch to 100-percent alternative energy—a monumental step in leadership, as it was the only company in New York County to make this full commitment. The decision was also a move toward reclaiming the Brooklyn waterfront from its industrial past and making it a more positive residential place. To this end, the brewery has spoken out against a proposal to build a power plant along the Brooklyn shore. For the Brooklyn Brewery, switching to alternative energy was a way to say "We believe there's another way."

It has signed a 15-year contract
to continue using wind energy and
even promotes Community Energy (the
company's alternative energy supplier)
on its coasters, providing the
company's contact details. To take
its positive practices one step
farther, the brewery's grain shafts
are picked up by local farmers to
provide their livestock with high-
quality feed, ensuring 100-percent
reuse of the company's waste.

01 Beer and ale varieties
02 Brooklyn Brewery facilities

ETHICAL PROCESS AND PRACTICE →

01

WHAT: T-shirts
WHO: American Apparel
WHERE: United States
MATERIALS: Cotton
QUALITIES: Ethical labor
practices, eco-friendly
materials

As a smart company with youth and style, the American Apparel (AA) brand is at the cutting edge with everyday fashion that is "sweatshop free." "We are trying to rediscover the essence of classic products like the basic T-shirt, once an icon of Western culture and freedom. Our goal is to make garments that people love to wear without having to rely on cheap labor." Refusing to exploit overseas manufacturing, AA's downtown Los Angeles factory is now considered the

largest sewn-products facility in the United States. The company's mission is for everyone touched personally by its business to have a positive experience. Sewing employees are paid at least roughly double the standard minimum wage, achieve better pay and promotion with experience, and have access to company-subsidized health insurance. AA also offers free English classes to its workers, massage therapists to work with factory workers, and rarely asks employees

to work longer than 8-hour days—a
huge difference from its overseas
competitors. AA's Sustainable Edition
offers certified organic cotton,
making its product eco-friendly, and
the company has also implemented a
program to recycle over a million
pounds of scrap fabric per year. AA's
success is testament to the fact that
social consciousness can be profitably
applied to many companies and
industries worldwide.

01 American Apparel tank top
02 American Apparel T-shirt
   and shorts

URBAN PARK →

01

WHAT: Endangered Garden
WHO: Patricia Johanson
WHERE: United States
MATERIALS: Various
QUALITIES: Eco-
supporting design

Known as an urban artist who creates
environmental sanctuaries in areas
that might otherwise be wastelands,
Johanson is a conceptual thinker,
visual architect, and biologist all
in one. Her urban designs flow from
intense research and planning.
Endangered Garden, a Johanson
creation, is a public park created
over what was once a sewage treatment
plant located on the edge of the San
Francisco Bay.

Johanson's designs take every life-
form into consideration and each
element serves to encourage the life
and growth of a unified ecosystem. In
Endangered Garden, the coiling snake
walkway serves as a refuge for small
vertebrates that might otherwise be
prey to crabs and fish. In turn, the
thriving existence of these species
serves to attract waterfowl that also
inhabit the area. The plants and
foliage chosen to populate the garden

provide food for the waterfowl and
protective coverings for the small
mammals. These plant species, which
may be rare or endangered themselves,
also attract other locally endangered
wildlife, such as the rare Pygmy Blue,
California's smallest butterfly.

This is the true beauty of Endangered
Garden, as well as Johanson's other
design work. Although humans will
appreciate these "natural

environments," we are not the sole
intended audience of their design.
Her public parks and gardens are truly
universal. The most minute organism
is given as much consideration as the
most obvious and dominant species—us.
In Johanson's work the ecosystem finds
harmony. "This is the real power of
my work: not how it 'looks,' but how
it 'acts'—how design can make a real
difference in the world beyond the
internal dialog of its practitioners."

01 Ribbon Worm / Tide Pools path
02 The plants chosen provide
   a haven for local butterflies

04

05

ARCHITECTURE MODELED ON NATURE→

01

WHAT: Tsui House
WHO: Tsui Design & Research Inc.
WHERE: United States
MATERIALS: Concrete, styrofoam/cement block, hardwall structural plaster, stucco, nontoxic waterproofing, acrylic, marine fiberglass, Douglas fir, recycled wood, birch veneer plywood, Opalina iridescent paint, exterior paint
QUALITIES: Innovative use of sustainable materials and design

Many of the great architects have looked at the way that nature "designs" as inspiration for their own creations. However, according to Dr. Eugene Tsui, others have referred to nature only in a strictly metaphorical and visual sense.

Tsui and his design team focus on examining the way that nature designs to translate that knowledge into the way humans design. Tsui's unique buildings seek to create extraordinary visual designs that protect and preserve the natural ecology of the

surrounding environment, as well as being self-sufficient. Economy of cost, conservation of labor, application of new, simplified construction methods, use of innovative materials and ecological technology, and extraordinary and striking designs are all fundamental features of Tsui's work.

The structure for the Tsui House is based upon the world's most indestructible living creature—the Tardigrade. With its oval plan and parabolic top, it utilizes the same

02

structural principles that nature
employs to create an astoundingly
durable building. Internationally
touted as the world's safest house,
it features an oval, reinforced
concrete foundation over a series of
large, perforated drainpipes, which
immediately expel any water that
builds up or emanates from the soil
or from sudden flood conditions. The
walls are constructed from a material
called Ener-grid Block. This is
lightweight, fireproof, waterproof,
and termiteproof, and is also very
resistant to earthquakes.

01 Tsui House
02 Tsui House window detail
03 Tsui House front entrance

01

152/153

WHAT: Reyes House
WHO: Tsui Design & Research Inc.
WHERE: United States
MATERIALS: Douglas Fir, plywood,
acrylic panels, marine fiberglass,
galvanized metal pipe, steel cable,
Structolite plaster, concrete,
steel pipe
QUALITIES: Innovative use of
sustainable materials and design

The form and function of the Reyes
House were directly inspired by the
dragonfly. Hinged roof ventilation
"wings," operated by hand cranks, open
up the roof at the occupants' wish,
creating what Tsui calls "living
architecture." With the introduction
of parts that move, architecture is
better able to respond to changing
requirements—like a living organism.

01 Reyes House roof structure
02 Reyes House

WALLPAPER →

01

WHAT: Paradise Project
WHO: Rinzen and
Weiden+Kennedy
WHERE: Australia,
The Netherlands
MATERIALS: Paper
QUALITIES: Thought-
provoking design

Rinzen is a collaborative design studio with a vibrant vision that "bends reality into shapes pleasing to the eye and ear." In a collaboration with design agency Weiden+Kennedy, Amsterdam, Rinzen was asked to create three unique patterns based on the Western world's perception of paradise and the reality of countries that offer it. The patterns are beautiful from afar, resembling the artwork of a Hawaiian shirt, but a closer look at the details reveals a second layer of meaning. Rinzen tackled the theme in three aspects: direct military destruction, socioeconomic/cultural impact, and environmental damage. The pieces were produced as continuous paper print, and installed as wallpaper at the Amsterdam offices of Weiden+Kennedy.

<u>BIOLUMINESCENT LIGHTING</u> →

01

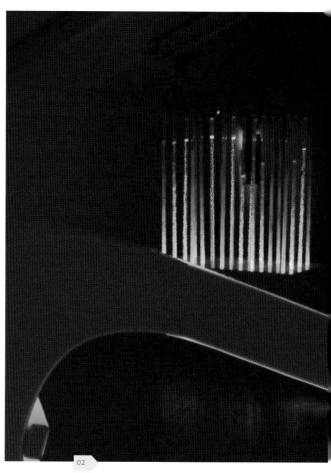

02

<u>WHAT: LuxCorp furniture</u>
<u>WHO: John Nicholson and</u>
<u>Dr. Kathy Takayama</u>
<u>WHERE: Australia</u>
<u>MATERIALS:</u>
<u>Bioluminescent</u>
<u>bacteria</u>
<u>QUALITIES: Use of</u>
<u>alternative energy,</u>
<u>thought-provoking design</u>

LuxCorp furniture is the result of a collaborative experiment in design and technology between microbiologist Dr. Kathy Takayama and visual artist John Nicholson. Together they created furniture that emits light through the harnessing of bioluminescent bacteria—bacteria that produce light as a result of an oxidation process. These colonies of bacteria illuminate, or power, the LuxCorp designs just as any other home object would be powered by regular electricity. The designs were created as prototypes for an exhibition on art and science entitled Metis. LuxCorp was designed to challenge people's perceptions about microbiology and its use within the world of design. Its creators see the illuminating possibilities unveiled not necessarily as an alternative form of energy, but as a new option for luxury lighting.

03

BATHING SYSTEM →

WHAT: reHOUSE/bath
WHO: Fulguro and Thomas
Jomini Architecture
Studio
WHERE: Switzerland
MATERIALS: Molded
synthetics, woven felt,
ceramic, oak
QUALITIES: Thought-
provoking design,
conserves water

Designed by Fulgaro, in collaboration with Thomas Jomini Architecture Studio, reHOUSE is a research platform for sustainable and ethical design. reHOUSE/bath is a new section of this platform, focusing on the bathroom as a biotope where nature and mankind interact. The objects that have been designed for this project are: BATH, reNET, reVAP, reSIZE, and reMAT.

BATH is a mobile bathing surface. To wash, the user has to sit on the bench that strides over the edge of the bath.

BATH's evacuation system is connected to a series of plants that drink the water used for the washing. The user must adapt his water consumption to the number of plants around him. The grown plants create an organic screen.

reVAP is a ceramic water collector. The amount of water you can use for washing depends upon the plants' ability to absorb it.

reNET, a connection piece, allows many
combinations for BATH and reVAP.

reSIZE is comprised of a natural sponge
to force the user to consume a minimum
amount of water. This allows only
rinsing—no bathing or showering. Every
bucket with a capacity greater than 5l
(10^{1}/$_{2}$pt) is perforated so that it can
only contain this amount of water.

reMAT is a natural felt mat. It
absorbs excess moisture from the air
after a rinsing and releases it during
the day.

01 BENCH and reSIZE
02 BATH, reMAP, reVAP
03 Exhibition display,
   Langenthal, Switzerland

DECORATED PLASTIC FURNITURE →

01

160/161

WHAT: Material Memories
WHO: Rob Thompson
WHERE: United Kingdom
MATERIALS: Found
materials, plastic
QUALITIES: Recycles found
materials, extends
product life span through
personal touch

Materials, memories, and our daily surroundings all influence the work of designer Rob Thompson. His project Material Memories combines surface ageing, technology, and our emotional bonding with products. The style and approach was heavily influenced by his experiences of growing up in Norfolk, England, in an Elizabethan, timber-framed cottage. By mixing "experienced" materials (those available for reuse such as waste or something more personal) with plastic, he creates a surface effect that will change over time as it is used. Taking advantage of the irregularities in the manufacturing process, each product is visually unique. Although mixing these materials inevitably makes the plastic used harder to recycle, the notion that product is meant to change with its owner over time, ideally creating an emotional bond, gives Material Memories an extended life span. In the end, the owner has a stool that is unmatched by any other and that will constantly evolve as the surface wears to expose more of its hidden materials.

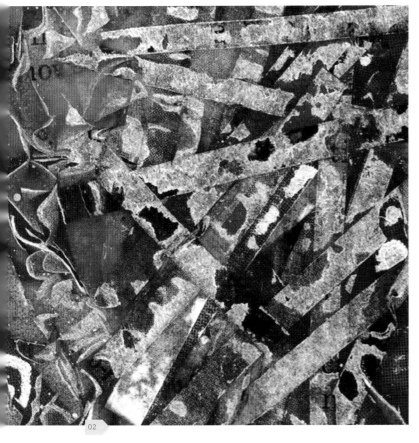

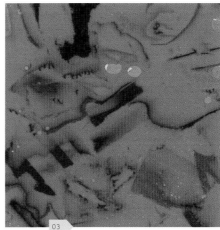

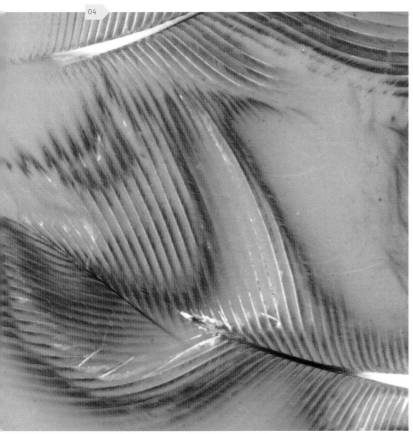

01 Material Memories stools
02 Worn paper detail
03 Paper detail
04 Feather detail

INFLATABLE FURNITURE →

01 SoftAir lounger
02 SoftAir furniture is light
   and easy to move
03 SoftAir footrests

162/163

WHAT: SoftAir
WHO: Jan Dranger
WHERE: Sweden
MATERIALS: Plastic
QUALITIES: Lightweight,
minimal use of materials

For Jan Dranger, making eco-friendly products that are readily available and appeal to the youth market is of great importance. The youth culture is what drives trends, so if sustainability is to become an integral part of culture and design, it must first be accepted by young people. SoftAir is a youthful and affordable furniture design that utilizes a 100-percent eco-friendly and absolutely free resource—air! A product of simplicity, functionality, and comfort, each item of SoftAir furniture comes packed flat. Self-assembly time is less than half an hour, using air from a hair dryer or vacuum cleaner. There is an array of colors and patterns to choose from and the covers can be removed and machine washed as often as necessary. SoftAir's material is surprisingly durable, and is hard-wearing enough to satisfy even the extremely strict requirements of Swedish Möbelfakta tests—recommendations normally reserved for heavy-duty use in public areas. The low raw material and handling costs, due to minimal components and space-saving packaging, are reflected in the low pricing.

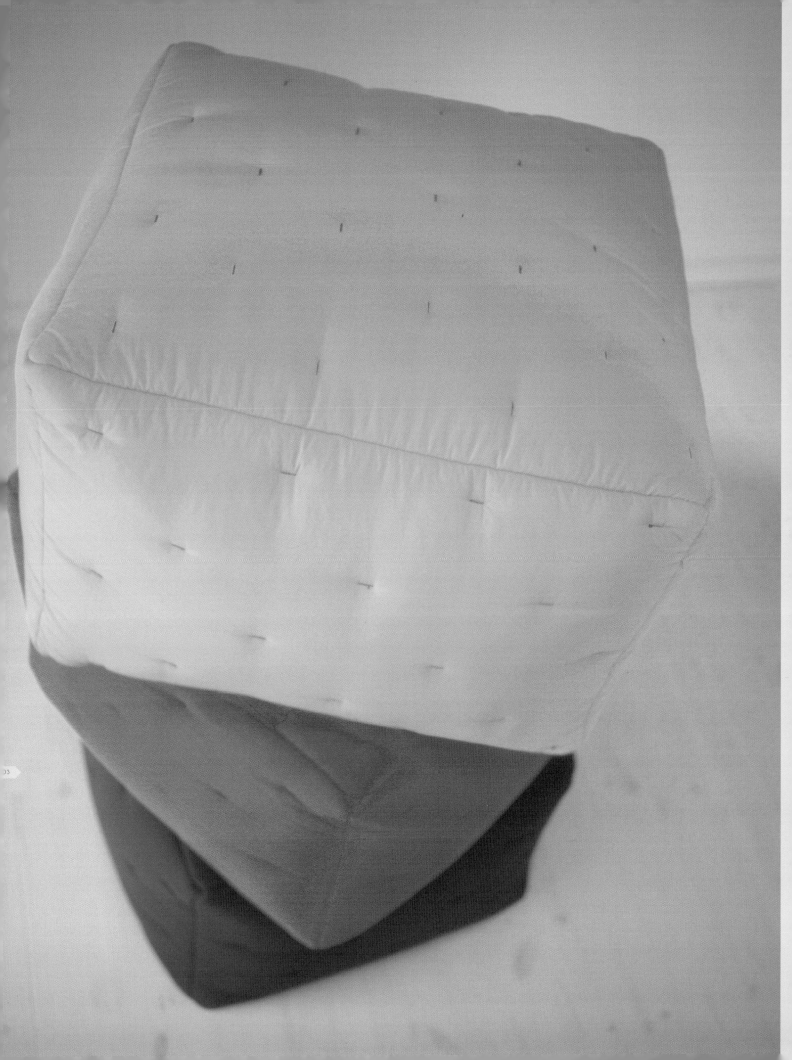

05—
FURTHER INFORMATION

Directory / Suppliers / Organizations and Sources of Information / Further Reading / Thanks / Index

DIRECTORY →

INTRODUCTION

Edwin Datschefski
United Kingdom
www.biothinking.com

TRANSFORMING MATERIALS

Alyce Santoro
Brooklyn, NY
United States
www.alycesantoro.com
www.sonicfabric.com

Annemette Beck
Lindehusvej 5
DK-5750 Ringe
Denmark
www.annemette-beck.dk

Bart Bettencourt
70 North 6th St
Brooklyn, NY 11211
United States
www.bettencourtwood.com

Bless
France/Germany
www.bless-service.de

Colin Reedy
MetaMorf
United States
www.metamorfdesign.com

Emiliano Godoy
Godoylab
Lopez Cotilla 1851-206
Col. del Valle
Mexico DF, 03100
Mexico
www.godoylab.com

Manuel Wijffels
Denovo Design
Gagelstraat 6-A
5611 BH EINDHOVEN
The Netherlands
www.denovo.nl

Michael Jantzen
United States
www.humanshelter.org

MIO
340 North 12th St, Unit 301
Philadelphia, PA 19107
United States
www.mioculture.com

Papcorn
Laurids Skaus Gade 15, 3 tv.
DK-2200 Cph. N
www.papcorn.dk

Peter Danko
Danko/Persing Enterprises
214 North Franklin St
Red Lion, PA 17356
United States
www.peterdanko.com

Remarkable
56 Glentham Rd
London SW13 9JJ
United Kingdom
www.remarkable.co.uk

Shigeru Ban Architects Tokyo
5-2-4 Matsubara, Setagaya
Tokyo 156-0043
Japan

Studio Rob
4 Canal Building
135 Shepherdess Walk
London N1 7RR
United Kingdom
www.studiorob.co.uk

Tom Dixon
The Shop, 28 All Saints Rd
London W11 1HG
United Kingdom
www.tomdixon.net

Ukao
United States
www.ukao.com

EFFICIENCY BY DESIGN

Artcoustic
6 Pickwick House
20 Ebenezer St
London N1 7NP
United Kingdom
www.artcoustic.com

Ben Wilson
United Kingdom
www.downlow.co.uk

Dave Kuene
Buro Vormkrijgers
The Netherlands
www.burovormkrijgers.nl
----

easyHotel
United Kingdom
www.easyhotel.com

Erik Newman
PO Box 477091,Chicago, Il 60647
United States
www.hhuman.com

In.Kitchen
www.whirlpool.com

Jan Dranger
Sweden
www.softair.com

Lot-ek
55 Little West 12th St
New York, NY 10014-1304
United States
www.lot-ek.com

Luceplan
315 Hudson St
New York, NY 10013
United States
www.luceplanusa.com

Pepper-mint
5 Albemarle Way
London EC1V 4JB
United Kingdon
www.pepper-mint.com

Peter Hancheck
New York, NY
United States
peter_hanchek@hotmail.com

Richard Hutten
PO Box 6005
NL-3002 AA Rotterdam
The Netherlands
www.richardhutten.com

Sean Godsell Architects
45 Flinders Lane
Melbourne, Vic 3000
Australia
www.seangodsell.com

Superhappybunny
United States
www.superhappybunny.com

TRUCK Product Architecture
United States
www.offi.com/
designers-truck.html

IMAGINATIVE REUSE

Carrie Collins
Fabric Horse
319 N. 11th St, 3rd Floor
Philadelphia, PA 19107
United States
www.fabrichorse.com

Colleen Rae Smiley
Brooklyn, NY 11211
United States
colleenraes@yahoo.com

Demano
Pallars 94, 7º 1ª
08018 Barcelona
Spain
www.demano.net

Ed van Hinte
The Netherlands
www.eternally-yours.org
www.survivinginternet.org

Eva Menz
United Kingdom
www.evamenz.com
----

nydesignroom
339 Bedford Ave
Brooklyn, NY 11211
United States
www.nydesignroom.com

Scrapile
70 North 6th St
Brooklyn, NY 11211
United States
www.bettencourtwood.com

Sonic Design
181 North 11 St
Brooklyn, NY 11211
United States
www.sonicny.com

Uroads
Italy
www.uroads.com

SUPPLIERS →

SOCIAL SENSIBILITY

Patrik Fredriksons
76 Trinity Court, Gray's Inn Rd
London WC1X 8JY
United Kingdom
www.patrikfredriksons.com

PAPER

----

www.curtisfinepapers.com
Large range of environmental
papers

American Apparel
United States
www.americanapparel.net

Brooklyn Brewery
United States
www.brooklynbrewery.com

Rinzen
Australia
www.rinzen.com

TIMBER

----

www.earthsourcewood.com
The EarthSource is a reliable
source of wood products that
originate from forests that are
certified for their sustainable
harvest practices

Ezio Manzini
Italy
ezio.manzini@polimi.it

Venture Snowboards
P.O. Box 1563
Durango, CO 81302
United States
www.venturesnowboards.com

Fulguro
Rue du Maupas 28
1004 Lausanne
Switzerland
www.fulguro.ch

----

www.ecotimber.co.uk
Ecotimber Ltd is an independent
company with more than 12 years'
experience in sourcing and
marketing timber that has been
produced in a way that is
environmentally appropriate,
socially beneficial, and
economically viable

The Future Perfect
115 North 6th Street
Brooklyn, NY 11211
www.thefutureperfect.com

LuxCorp
Australia
Kathy Takayama
k.takayama@unsw.edu.au
John Nicholson
j.nicholson@unsw.edu.au

Method Products, Inc.
30 Hotaling Place, 3rd floor
San Francisco, CA 94111
United States
www.methodhome.com

Modern Organic Products
United States
www.mopproducts.com

Office of Mobile Design
1725 Abbot Kinney Blvd
Venice, CA 90291
United States
www.designmobile.com

Patricia Johanson
United States
www.patriciajohanson.com

ORGANIZATIONS AND SOURCES OF INFORMATION →

ARCHITECTURE
----

www.spaceagency.ca
A committee of The Vancouver
League for Studies in
Architecture and the Environment

BUSINESS AND WASTE MANAGEMENT
----

www.designgreen.org
Design:Green aims to transform
business by showing the way
toward products that are at
once sustainable, innovative,
profitable, and able to compete
in the global marketplace
----

www.forumforthefuture.org.uk
Forum for the Future is a
leading sustainable development
charity. It promotes and
educates different groups
in sustainable development
----

www.globalff.org
The Global Futures Foundation
runs conferences on Industrial
Ecology, and has many examples
of current ethical and
sustainable practices
----

www.greenstreets.ie
Consultancy firm offering
training, financial, and waste
management services
----

www.indsoc.com
The Industrial Society is a
campaigning body that promotes
progressive agendas for
industrial enterprise in Europe
----

www.ilsr.org
The Institute for Local Self-
Reliance (ILSR) is a nonprofit
research and educational
organization that provides
technical assistance and
information on environmentally
sound economic development
strategies
----

www.tbli.org
Brooklyn Bridge is a knowledge
broker specializing in social
responsibility. They make
connections for companies and
individuals from the old to the
new sustainable economy, by
utilizing their extensive global
network. The focus is finance

**www.uneptie.org/pc/pc/tools/
ecodesign.htm**
UNEP seek to promote and
facilitate discussion, networks,
and action for more sustainable
products and services
----

www.zeri.org
The Zero Emissions Research
Institute focuses on zero-waste
industrial technology

DESIGN

www.ce.cmu.edu/GreenDesign/
The Green Design Institute is a
major interdisciplinary research
effort to make an impact on
environmental quality through
green design

**www.cfd.rmit.edu.au/dfe/
cfd_2_5.html**
Case studies from the Royal
Melbourne Institute of
Technology's EcoRedesign program
----

www.cfsd.org.uk
The Centre For Sustainable
Design facilitates discussion
and research on eco-design
and broader sustainability
considerations in product and
service development
----

www.designresource.org
This design organization is
committed to the development of
new materials and sustainable
design in product design and
architecture
----

www.designinsite.dk
Design inSite provides the tools
for designers to evaluate the
whole lifecycle of a product, and
the environmental properties of
the materials and processes used

**www.io.tudelft.nl/research/dfs/
idemat/index.htm**
The IDEMAT database was
developed by the Delft
University of Technology as
a source of environmental
information on materials
and processes

**www.metropolismag.com/cda/
sustainable.php**
Sustainable Metropolis is an
online magazine dedicated to
issues of sustainable design.
It includes listings of new
products, case studies, courses,
resources, and sustainable events
----

www.o2.org
International network of
eco-designers, with links to
interesting sources and ideas

ENVIRONMENT

----

www.cat.org.uk
CAT is an environmental charity aiming to "inspire, inform, and enable" people to live more sustainably

----

www.ends.co.uk
Environmental Data Services provides information on issues and events for environmental professionals

----

www.enn.com
The Environmental News Network focuses on issues that shape the environment

----

www.greenmap.org
The Green Map System (GMS) promotes sustainability and community participation in the local natural and built environment. It facilitates the progress of communities around the world toward ecological and cultural sustainability

----

www.greenpeace.org.uk
Greenpeace uses nonviolent, creative confrontation to expose global environmental problems and their causes. They research solutions and alternatives to help provide a path for a green and peaceful future

----

www.grist.org
Grist Magazine is an online environmental magazine. Features include Q & A with activists, book reviews, and an environmental advice column

----

GLASS

----

www.glasspac.com
Glasspac provides information on glass as a packaging material

----

www.gpi.org/Recycling.html
The Glass Packaging Institute is at the forefront of glass container recycling efforts

----

PLASTICS

----

www.plasticsresource.com
Provides information on plastics and the environment, conservation, and recycling

----

www.plasticx.com
Provides a worldwide information exchange service for scrap plastic recycling

----

TIMBER

----

www.certifiedwood.org
The Certified Forest Products Council (CFPC) promotes forest certification as a tool to conserve, and restore, the world's forests

----

www.efi.fi
The European Forest Institute is the leading forest research network in Europe

----

www.fsc-uk.info
The Forest Stewardship Council promotes responsible management of the world's forests. There are national working groups in 28 countries

----

www.wcmc.org.uk/trees
An information service on tree conservation; provides information on the conservation status of tree species worldwide

----

FURTHER READING →

ARCHITECTURE

----

*Big and Green: Toward
Sustainable Architecture in
the 21st Century*
David Gissen

----

*Mobile: The Art of Portable
Architecture*
Jennifer Siegal

----

*Rural Studio: Samuel Mockbee and
an Architecture of Decency*
Andrea Oppenheimer, Timothy
Hursley

----

*Eternally Yours: Visions on
Product Endurance*
Ed van Hinte

----

*Natural Capitalism: Creating
the next Industrial Revolution*
Paul Hawken, Amary Lovins,
L. Hunter Lovins

DESIGN

----

*The Complete Guide to
Eco-Friendly Design*
Poppy Evans

----

*Cradle to Cradle: Remaking the
Way We Make Things*
William McDonough and Michael
Braungart

----

*Droog Design: Spirit of the
Nineties*
Renny Ramakers, Gijs Bakker

----

*Eco: An Essential Sourcebook for
Environmentally Friendly Design
and Decoration*
Elizabeth Wilhide

----

*Eco Deco: Chic, Ecological
Design Using Recycled Materials*
Stewart and Sally Walton

----

*The Eco-design Handbook:
A Complete Sourcebook for
the Home and Office*
Alastair Fuad-Luke

Ecodesign Navigator
Matthew Simon, et al

EcoDesign: The Sourcebook
Alastair Fuad-Luke

IDEO: Masters of Innovation
Jeremy Myerson

----

*Less + More: Droog Design
in Context*
Renny Ramakers

----

*The Total Beauty of Sustainable
Products*
Edwin Datschefski

----

*Tresspassers: Inspirations for
Eco-efficient Design*
Conny Bakker, Ed van Hinte

ENVIRONMENT

----

*Ecovention: Current Art to
Transform Ecologies*
Sue Spaid

----

*Green Design: Design for the
Environment*
Dorothy Mackenzie

----

*The Green Imperative: Natural
Design for the Real World*
Victor Papanek

----

*Lightness: The Inevitable
Renaissance of Minimum Energy
Structures*
Adriaan Beukers, Ed van Hinte

THANKS →

Thank you to all the contributors
for their patience, information,
and enthusiasm. Thank you to all
the people who worked to create
this book—directly and indirectly—
and to friends, and family.

Index